MznLnx

Missing Links Exam Preps

Exam Prep for

Marketing Research

Parasuraman, Grewal, Krishnan, 1st Edition

The MznLnx Exam Prep is your link from the texbook and lecture to your exams.
The MznLnx Exam Preps are unauthorized and comprehensive reviews of your textbooks.

All material provided by MznLnx and Rico Publications (c) 2010
Textbook publishers and textbook authors do not particpate in or contribute to these reviews.

MznLnx

Rico Publications

Exam Prep for Marketing Research
1st Edition
Parasuraman, Grewal, Krishnan

Publisher: Raymond Houge
Assistant Editor: Michael Rouger
Text and Cover Designer: Lisa Buckner
Marketing Manager: Sara Swagger
Project Manager, Editorial Production: Jerry Emerson
Art Director: Vernon Lowerui

Product Manager: Dave Mason
Editorial Assitant: Rachel Guzmanji
Pedagogy: Debra Long
Cover Image: Jim Reed/Getty Images
Text and Cover Printer: City Printing, Inc.
Compositor: Media Mix, Inc.

(c) 2010 Rico Publications

ALL RIGHTS RESERVED. No part of this work covered by the copyright may be reproduced or used in any form or by an means--graphic, electronic, or mechanical, including photocopying, recording, taping, Web distribution, information storage, and retrieval systems, or in any other manner--without the written permission of the publisher.

Printed in the United States
ISBN:

For more information about our products, contact us at:
Dave.Mason@RicoPublications.com

For permission to use material from this text or product, submit a request online to:
Dave.Mason@RicoPublications.com

Contents

CHAPTER 1
The Nature and Scope of Marketing Research — 1

CHAPTER 2
The Marketing Research Process — 11

CHAPTER 3
Types of Marketing Research — 22

CHAPTER 4
Secondary Data — 28

CHAPTER 5
Using Geographic Information Systems for Marketing Research — 35

CHAPTER 6
Primary-Data Collection — 41

CHAPTER 7
Qualitative Research — 51

CHAPTER 8
Experimentation in Marketing Research — 58

CHAPTER 9
Measurement and Scaling — 69

CHAPTER 10
Questionnaire Design — 77

CHAPTER 11
Sampling Foundations — 81

CHAPTER 12
Quality Control and Initial Analysis of Data — 88

CHAPTER 13
Hypothesis Testing — 95

CHAPTER 14
Examining Associations: Correlation and Regression — 105

CHAPTER 15
Overview of Other Multivariate Techniques — 110

CHAPTER 16
Presenting Research Results — 119

ANSWER KEY — 124

TO THE STUDENT

COMPREHENSIVE

The *MznLnx* Exam Prep series is designed to help you pass your exams. Editors at MznLnx review your textbooks and then prepare these practice exams to help you master the textbook material. Unlike study guides, workbooks, and practice tests provided by the texbook publisher and textbook authors, *MznLnx* gives you **all** of the material in each chapter in exam form, not just samples, so you can be sure to nail your exam.

MECHANICAL

The MznLnx Exam Prep series creates exams that will help you learn the subject matter as well as test you on your understanding. Each question is designed to help you master the concept. Just working through the exams, you gain an understanding of the subject--its a simple mechanical process that produces success.

INTEGRATED STUDY GUIDE AND REVIEW

MznLnx is not just a set of exams designed to test you, its also a comprehensive review of the subject content. Each exam question is also a review of the concept, making sure that you will get the answer correct without having to go to other sources of material. You learn as you go! Its the easiest way to pass an exam.

HUMOR

Studying can be tedious and dry. MznLnx's instructional design includes moderate humor within the exam questions on occassion, to break the tedium and revitalize the brain

Chapter 1. The Nature and Scope of Marketing Research

1. In economics, an externality or spillover of an economic transaction is an impact on a party that is not directly involved in the transaction. In such a case, prices do not reflect the full costs or benefits in production or consumption of a product or service. A positive impact is called an _____ benefit, while a negative impact is called an _____ cost.
   - a. ADTECH
   - b. ACNielsen
   - c. AMAX
   - d. External

2. The Oxford University Press defines _____ as 'marketing on a worldwide scale reconciling or taking commercial advantage of global operational differences, similarities and opportunities in order to meet global objectives.' Oxford University Press' Glossary of Marketing Terms.

   Here are three reasons for the shift from domestic to _____ as given by the authors of the textbook, _____ Management--3rd Edition by Masaaki Kotabe and Kristiaan Helsen, 2004.

   One of the product categories in which global competition has been easy to track is in U.S. automotive sales.

   - a. Diversity marketing
   - b. Digital marketing
   - c. Guerrilla Marketing
   - d. Global marketing

3. _____ refers to the production of some commodity or service, such as a television program, using a company's own funds, staff, or resources.

   This is in contrast to production being outsourced (contracted out) to another company.

   - Proprietary

   - a. Intangible assets
   - b. Outsourcing
   - c. ACNielsen
   - d. In-house

4. _____ is defined by the American _____ Association as the activity, set of institutions, and processes for creating, communicating, delivering, and exchanging offerings that have value for customers, clients, partners, and society at large. The term developed from the original meaning which referred literally to going to market, as in shopping, or going to a market to sell goods or services.

   _____ practice tends to be seen as a creative industry, which includes advertising, distribution and selling.

   - a. Marketing myopia
   - b. Product naming
   - c. Customer acquisition management
   - d. Marketing

5. The _____ is generally accepted as the use and specification of the four p's describing the strategic position of a product in the marketplace. One version of the origins of the _____ starts in 1948 when James Culliton said that a marketing decision should be a result of something similar to a recipe. This version continued in 1953 when Neil Borden, in his American Marketing Association presidential address, took the recipe idea one step further and coined the term 'Marketing-Mix'.
   - a. 180SearchAssistant
   - b. 6-3-5 Brainwriting
   - c. Power III
   - d. Marketing mix

Chapter 1. The Nature and Scope of Marketing Research

6. Consumer market research is a form of applied sociology that concentrates on understanding the behaviours, whims and preferences, of consumers in a market-based economy, and aims to understand the effects and comparative success of marketing campaigns. The field of consumer _____ as a statistical science was pioneered by Arthur Nielsen with the founding of the ACNielsen Company in 1923 .

Thus _____ is the systematic and objective identification, collection, analysis, and dissemination of information for the purpose of assisting management in decision making related to the identification and solution of problems and opportunities in marketing.

   a. Marketing research process
   b. Focus group
   c. Logit analysis
   d. Marketing research

7. _____ can be regarded as an outcome of mental processes (cognitive process) leading to the selection of a course of action among several alternatives. Every _____ process produces a final choice. The output can be an action or an opinion of choice.
   a. Power III
   b. 180SearchAssistant
   c. 6-3-5 Brainwriting
   d. Decision making

8. A _____ is a written document that details the necessary actions to achieve one or more marketing objectives. It can be for a product or service, a brand, or a product line. _____s cover between one and five years.
   a. Marketing plan
   b. Disruptive technology
   c. Prosumer
   d. Marketing strategy

9. A _____ is a process that can allow an organization to concentrate its limited resources on the greatest opportunities to increase sales and achieve a sustainable competitive advantage. A _____ should be centered around the key concept that customer satisfaction is the main goal.

A _____ is most effective when it is an integral component of corporate strategy, defining how the organization will successfully engage customers, prospects, and competitors in the market arena.

   a. Marketing strategy
   b. Cyberdoc
   c. Psychographic
   d. Societal marketing

10. _____ is an organization's process of defining its strategy and making decisions on allocating its resources to pursue this strategy, including its capital and people. Various business analysis techniques can be used in _____, including SWOT analysis (Strengths, Weaknesses, Opportunities, and Threats) and PEST analysis (Political, Economic, Social, and Technological analysis) or STEER analysis involving Socio-cultural, Technological, Economic, Ecological, and Regulatory factors and EPISTEL (Environment, Political, Informatic, Social, Technological, Economic and Legal)

_____ is the formal consideration of an organization's future course. All _____ deals with at least one of three key questions:

   1. 'What do we do?'
   2. 'For whom do we do it?'
   3. 'How do we excel?'

In business _____, the third question is better phrased 'How can we beat or avoid competition?'. (Bradford and Duncan, page 1.)

a. 6-3-5 Brainwriting
c. 180SearchAssistant
b. Power III
d. Strategic planning

11. _____ in organizations and public policy is both the organizational process of creating and maintaining a plan; and the psychological process of thinking about the activities required to create a desired goal on some scale. As such, it is a fundamental property of intelligent behavior. This thought process is essential to the creation and refinement of a plan, or integration of it with other plans, that is, it combines forecasting of developments with the preparation of scenarios of how to react to them.

a. 6-3-5 Brainwriting
c. Power III
b. 180SearchAssistant
d. Planning

12. A _____ is a plan of action designed to achieve a particular goal.

_____ is different from tactics. In military terms, tactics is concerned with the conduct of an engagement while _____ is concerned with how different engagements are linked.

a. Strategy
c. 180SearchAssistant
b. Power III
d. 6-3-5 Brainwriting

13. A _____ is the space, actual or metaphorical, in which a market operates. The term is also used in a trademark law context to denote the actual consumer environment, ie. the 'real world' in which products and services are provided and consumed.

a. 180SearchAssistant
c. Power III
b. 6-3-5 Brainwriting
d. Marketplace

14. _____ refer to a collection of facts usually collected as the result of experience, observation or experiment or a set of premises. This may consist of numbers, words particularly as measurements or observations of a set of variables. _____ are often viewed as a lowest level of abstraction from which information and knowledge are derived.

a. Mean
c. Sample size
b. Data
d. Pearson product-moment correlation coefficient

15. _____ is systematic determination of merit, worth, and significance of something or someone using criteria against a set of standards. _____ often is used to characterize and appraise subjects of interest in a wide range of human enterprises, including the arts, criminal justice, foundations and non-profit organizations, government, health care, and other human services.

Depending on the topic of interest, there are professional groups which look to the quality and rigor of the _____ process.

a. ADTECH
c. ACNielsen
b. AMAX
d. Evaluation

Chapter 1. The Nature and Scope of Marketing Research

16. _____ describes the situation when output from (or information about the result of) an event or phenomenon in the past will influence the same event/phenomenon in the present or future. When an event is part of a chain of cause-and-effect that forms a circuit or loop, then the event is said to 'feed back' into itself.

_____ is also a synonym for:

- _____ Signal; the information about the initial event that is the basis for subsequent modification of the event.
- _____ Loop; the causal path that leads from the initial generation of the _____ signal to the subsequent modification of the event.

_____ is a mechanism, process or signal that is looped back to control a system within itself. Such a loop is called a _____ loop.

a. 6-3-5 Brainwriting
b. 180SearchAssistant
c. Feedback
d. Power III

17. _____ is either an activity of a living being (such as a human), consisting of receiving knowledge of the outside world through the senses, or the recording of data using scientific instruments. The term may also refer to any datum collected during this activity.

The scientific method requires _____s of nature to formulate and test hypotheses.

a. ACNielsen
b. Observation
c. AMAX
d. ADTECH

18. Combining Existing _____ Sources with New Primary Data Sources

Imagine that we could get hold of a good collection of surveys taken in earlier years, such as detailed studies about changes going on in this phase and hopefully additional studies in the years to come. Analyzing this data base over time could give us a good picture of what changes actually have taken place in the orientation of the population and of the extent to which new technical concepts did have an impact on subgroups of the population. Furthermore, data archives can help to prepare studies on change over time by monitoring what questions have been asked in earlier years and alerting principal investigators to important questions which should be repeated in planned research projects.

a. 180SearchAssistant
b. Secondary data
c. Power III
d. 6-3-5 Brainwriting

19. _____ generally refers to a list of all planned expenses and revenues. It is a plan for saving and spending. A _____ is an important concept in microeconomics, which uses a _____ line to illustrate the trade-offs between two or more goods.

a. 6-3-5 Brainwriting
b. 180SearchAssistant
c. Power III
d. Budget

20. _____ was originally coined by Austrian psychologist Alfred Adler in 1929. The current broader sense of the word dates from 1961.

In sociology, a _____ is the way a person lives.

a. Lifestyle
b. 180SearchAssistant
c. Power III
d. 6-3-5 Brainwriting

21. _____ is a set of six steps which defines the tasks to be accomplished in conducting a marketing research study. These include problem definition, developing an approach to problem, research design formulation, field work, data preparation and analysis, and report generation and presentation.

a. Market analysis
b. Simple random sampling
c. Preference-rank translation
d. Marketing research process

22. In economic models, the _____ time frame assumes no fixed factors of production. Firms can enter or leave the marketplace, and the cost (and availability) of land, labor, raw materials, and capital goods can be assumed to vary. In contrast, in the short-run time frame, certain factors are assumed to be fixed, because there is not sufficient time for them to change.

a. 180SearchAssistant
b. 6-3-5 Brainwriting
c. Power III
d. Long-run

23. _____, fundamental research (sometimes pure research), is research carried out to increase understanding of fundamental principles. Many times the end results have no direct or immediate commercial benefits, which is to say that _____ can be thought of as arising out of pure curiosity. However, in the long term it is the basis for many commercial products and applied research.

a. Reference value
b. Power III
c. Response rate
d. Basic research

24. _____, a business term, is a measure of how products and services supplied by a company meet or surpass customer expectation. It is seen as a key performance indicator within business and is part of the four perspectives of a Balanced Scorecard.

In a competitive marketplace where businesses compete for customers, _____ is seen as a key differentiator and increasingly has become a key element of business strategy.

a. Psychological pricing
b. Supplier diversity
c. Customer base
d. Customer satisfaction

25. _____, in strategic management and marketing, is the percentage or proportion of the total available market or market segment that is being serviced by a company. It can be expressed as a company's sales revenue (from that market) divided by the total sales revenue available in that market. It can also be expressed as a company's unit sales volume (in a market) divided by the total volume of units sold in that market.

a. Market share
b. Cyberdoc
c. Customer relationship management
d. Demand generation

26. In statistics, analysis of variance (_____) is a collection of statistical models, and their associated procedures, in which the observed variance is partitioned into components due to different explanatory variables. In its simplest form _____ gives a statistical test of whether the means of several groups are all equal, and therefore generalizes Student's two-sample t-test to more than two groups.

There are three conceptual classes of such models:

1. Fixed-effects models assumes that the data came from normal populations which may differ only in their means. (Model 1)
2. Random effects models assume that the data describe a hierarchy of different populations whose differences are constrained by the hierarchy. (Model 2)
3. Mixed-effect models describe situations where both fixed and random effects are present. (Model 3)

In practice, there are several types of _____ depending on the number of treatments and the way they are applied to the subjects in the experiment:

- One-way _____ is used to test for differences among two or more independent groups. Typically, however, the one-way _____ is used to test for differences among at least three groups, since the two-group case can be covered by a T-test (Gossett, 1908.)

a. ACNielsen
b. ADTECH
c. AMAX
d. ANOVA

27. _____ or _____ data refers to selected population characteristics as used in government, marketing or opinion research, or the _____ profiles used in such research. Note the distinction from the term 'demography' Commonly-used _____ include race, age, income, disabilities, mobility (in terms of travel time to work or number of vehicles available), educational attainment, home ownership, employment status, and even location.

a. Albert Einstein
b. African Americans
c. AStore
d. Demographic

28. _____ refers to selected population characteristics as used in government, marketing or opinion research, or the demographic profiles used in such research. Note the distinction from the term 'demography' Commonly-used demographics include race, age, income, disabilities, mobility (in terms of travel time to work or number of vehicles available), educational attainment, home ownership, employment status, and even location.

a. African Americans
b. AStore
c. Demographic data
d. Albert Einstein

29. _____ is the practice of individuals including commercial businesses, governments and institutions, facilitating the sale of their products or services to other companies or organizations that in turn resell them, use them as components in products or services they offer _____ is also called business-to-_____ for short. (Note that while marketing to government entities shares some of the same dynamics of organizational marketing, B2G Marketing is meaningfully different.)

a. Business marketing
b. Disruptive technology
c. Law of disruption
d. Mass marketing

Chapter 1. The Nature and Scope of Marketing Research   7

30. A _____ applies the scientific method to experimentally examine an intervention in the real world (or as many experimental economists like to say, naturally-occurring environments) rather than in the laboratory. _____s, like lab experiments, generally randomize subjects (or other sampling units) into treatment and control groups and compare outcomes between these groups. Clinical trials of pharmaceuticals are one example of _____s.
   a. Response variable
   b. Field experiment
   c. Power III
   d. 180SearchAssistant

31. _____ is a broad label that refers to any individuals or households that use goods and services generated within the economy. The concept of a _____ is used in different contexts, so that the usage and significance of the term may vary.

   A _____ is a person who uses any product or service.

   a. 180SearchAssistant
   b. 6-3-5 Brainwriting
   c. Consumer
   d. Power III

32. _____, in microeconomics, are the cost advantages that a business obtains due to expansion. They are factors that cause a producer's average cost per unit to fall as output rises. Diseconomies of scale are the opposite.
   a. Economies of scale
   b. ADTECH
   c. ACNielsen
   d. AMAX

33. _____ is a field of inquiry that crosscuts disciplines and subject matters. _____ers aim to gather an in-depth understanding of human behavior and the reasons that govern such behavior. The discipline investigates the why and how of decision making, not just what, where, when.
   a. 6-3-5 Brainwriting
   b. 180SearchAssistant
   c. Qualitative research
   d. Power III

34. _____ is a form of communication that typically attempts to persuade potential customers to purchase or to consume more of a particular brand of product or service. 'While now central to the contemporary global economy and the reproduction of global production networks, it is only quite recently that _____ has been more than a marginal influence on patterns of sales and production. The formation of modern _____ was intimately bound up with the emergence of new forms of monopoly capitalism around the end of the 19th and beginning of the 20th century as one element in corporate strategies to create, organize and where possible control markets, especially for mass produced consumer goods.
   a. AMAX
   b. ADTECH
   c. ACNielsen
   d. Advertising

35. _____ is the process of finding associated geographic coordinates (often expressed as latitude and longitude) from other geographic data, such as street addresses or the coordinates can be embedded into media such as digital photographs via geotagging.

   Reverse _____ is the opposite: finding an associated textual location such as a street address, from geographic coordinates.

   a. Power III
   b. 180SearchAssistant
   c. 6-3-5 Brainwriting
   d. Geocoding

36. An _____ is the manufacturing of a good or service within a category. Although _____ is a broad term for any kind of economic production, in economics and urban planning _____ is a synonym for the secondary sector, which is a type of economic activity involved in the manufacturing of raw materials into goods and products.

There are four key industrial economic sectors: the primary sector, largely raw material extraction industries such as mining and farming; the secondary sector, involving refining, construction, and manufacturing; the tertiary sector, which deals with services (such as law and medicine) and distribution of manufactured goods; and the quaternary sector, a relatively new type of knowledge _____ focusing on technological research, design and development such as computer programming, and biochemistry.

    a. ADTECH
    c. AMAX
    b. ACNielsen
    d. Industry

37. _____ is an advertisement in which a particular product specifically mentions a competitor by name for the express purpose of showing why the competitor is inferior to the product naming it.

This should not be confused with parody advertisements, where a fictional product is being advertised for the purpose of poking fun at the particular advertisement, nor should it be confused with the use of a coined brand name for the purpose of comparing the product without actually naming an actual competitor. ('Wikipedia tastes better and is less filling than the Encyclopedia Galactica.')

In the 1980s, during what has been referred to as the cola wars, soft-drink manufacturer Pepsi ran a series of advertisements where people, caught on hidden camera, in a blind taste test, chose Pepsi over rival Coca-Cola.

    a. Comparative advertising
    c. Heavy-up
    b. Cost per conversion
    d. GL-70

38. Advertising mail junk mail is the delivery of advertising material to recipients of postal mail. The delivery of advertising mail forms a large and growing service for many postal services, and _____ marketing forms a significant portion of the direct marketing industry. Some organizations attempt to help people opt-out of receiving advertising mail, in many cases motivated by a concern over its negative environmental impact.

    a. Directory Harvest Attack
    c. Telemarketing
    b. Phishing
    d. Direct mail

39. _____ is a term used to describe a process of preparing and collecting data - for example as part of a process improvement or similar project.

_____ usually takes place early on in an improvement project, and is often formalised through a _____ Plan which often contains the following activity.

1. Pre collection activity - Agree goals, target data, definitions, methods
2. Collection - _____
3. Present Findings - usually involves some form of sorting analysis and/or presentation.

A formal _____ process is necessary as it ensures that data gathered is both defined and accurate and that subsequent decisions based on arguments embodied in the findings are valid. The process provides both a baseline from which to measure from and in certain cases a target on what to improve. Types of _____ 1-By mail questionnaires 2-By personal interview

- Six sigma
- Sampling (statistics)

a. Power III
c. 180SearchAssistant
b. 6-3-5 Brainwriting
d. Data collection

40. A _____ is a structured collection of records or data that is stored in a computer system. The structure is achieved by organizing the data according to a _____ model. The model in most common use today is the relational model.
a. Power III
c. 6-3-5 Brainwriting
b. 180SearchAssistant
d. Database

41. _____ is a measure of the strength of a brand, product, service relative to competitive offerings. There is often a geographic element to the competitive landscape. In defining _____, you must see to what extent a product, brand, or firm controls a product category in a given geographic area.
a. Market system
c. Productivity
b. Discretionary spending
d. Market dominance

42. _____ is marketing based on relationship and value. It may be used to market a service or a product.

Marketing a service-base business is different from marketing a goods-base business.

a. 180SearchAssistant
c. Services Marketing
b. Power III
d. 6-3-5 Brainwriting

43. _____, in marketing and sales, is the collection of media used to support the sales of a product or service. These sales aids are intended to make the sales effort easier and more effective. The brand of the company usually presents itself by way of its collateral to enhance its brand.
a. Product churning
c. 180SearchAssistant
b. Power III
d. Marketing collateral

44. A _____ or trade mark, identified by the symbols ™ (not yet registered) and ® (registered) business organization or other legal entity to identify that the products and/or services to consumers with which the _____ appears originate from a unique source of origin, and to distinguish its products or services from those of other entities. A _____ is a type of intellectual property, and typically a name, word, phrase, logo, symbol, design, image, or a combination of these elements. There is also a range of non-conventional _____s comprising marks which do not fall into these standard categories.
a. Risk management
c. Trademark
b. 180SearchAssistant
d. Power III

Chapter 1. The Nature and Scope of Marketing Research

45. A supply chain is the system of organizations, people, technology, activities, information and resources involved in moving a product or service from _____ to customer. Supply chain activities transform natural resources, raw materials and components into a finished product that is delivered to the end customer. In sophisticated supply chain systems, used products may re-enter the supply chain at any point where residual value is recyclable.
   a. Product line extension
   b. Rebate
   c. Supplier
   d. Bringin' Home the Oil

46. In economics, business, retail, and accounting, a _____ is the value of money that has been used up to produce something, and hence is not available for use anymore. In economics, a _____ is an alternative that is given up as a result of a decision. In business, the _____ may be one of acquisition, in which case the amount of money expended to acquire it is counted as _____.
   a. Variable cost
   b. Fixed costs
   c. Cost
   d. Transaction cost

47. _____ in economics and business is the result of an exchange and from that trade we assign a numerical monetary value to a good, service or asset. If I trade 4 apples for an orange, the _____ of an orange is 4 - apples. Inversely, the _____ of an apple is 1/4 oranges.
   a. Contribution margin-based pricing
   b. Price
   c. Discounts and allowances
   d. Pricing

Chapter 2. The Marketing Research Process

1. A _____ is a collection of symbols, experiences and associations connected with a product, a service, a person or any other artifact or entity.

_____s have become increasingly important components of culture and the economy, now being described as 'cultural accessories and personal philosophies'.

Some people distinguish the psychological aspect of a _____ from the experiential aspect.

- a. Brandable software
- b. Store brand
- c. Brand equity
- d. Brand

2. _____ refer to a collection of facts usually collected as the result of experience, observation or experiment or a set of premises. This may consist of numbers, words particularly as measurements or observations of a set of variables. _____ are often viewed as a lowest level of abstraction from which information and knowledge are derived.

- a. Data
- b. Mean
- c. Pearson product-moment correlation coefficient
- d. Sample size

3. _____ is a process of gathering, modeling, and transforming data with the goal of highlighting useful information, suggesting conclusions, and supporting decision making. _____ has multiple facets and approaches, encompassing diverse techniques under a variety of names, in different business, science, and social science domains.

Data mining is a particular _____ technique that focuses on modeling and knowledge discovery for predictive rather than purely descriptive purposes.

- a. Data analysis
- b. 180SearchAssistant
- c. 6-3-5 Brainwriting
- d. Power III

4. In economics, an externality or spillover of an economic transaction is an impact on a party that is not directly involved in the transaction. In such a case, prices do not reflect the full costs or benefits in production or consumption of a product or service. A positive impact is called an _____ benefit, while a negative impact is called an _____ cost.

- a. ACNielsen
- b. ADTECH
- c. AMAX
- d. External

5. _____ was originally coined by Austrian psychologist Alfred Adler in 1929. The current broader sense of the word dates from 1961.

In sociology, a _____ is the way a person lives.

- a. 180SearchAssistant
- b. 6-3-5 Brainwriting
- c. Lifestyle
- d. Power III

6. _____ is defined by the American _____ Association as the activity, set of institutions, and processes for creating, communicating, delivering, and exchanging offerings that have value for customers, clients, partners, and society at large. The term developed from the original meaning which referred literally to going to market, as in shopping, or going to a market to sell goods or services.

_____ practice tends to be seen as a creative industry, which includes advertising, distribution and selling.

a. Marketing myopia
b. Marketing
c. Customer acquisition management
d. Product naming

7. Consumer market research is a form of applied sociology that concentrates on understanding the behaviours, whims and preferences, of consumers in a market-based economy, and aims to understand the effects and comparative success of marketing campaigns. The field of consumer _____ as a statistical science was pioneered by Arthur Nielsen with the founding of the ACNielsen Company in 1923.

Thus _____ is the systematic and objective identification, collection, analysis, and dissemination of information for the purpose of assisting management in decision making related to the identification and solution of problems and opportunities in marketing.

a. Focus group
b. Logit analysis
c. Marketing research process
d. Marketing research

8. The Oxford University Press defines _____ as 'marketing on a worldwide scale reconciling or taking commercial advantage of global operational differences, similarities and opportunities in order to meet global objectives.' Oxford University Press' Glossary of Marketing Terms.

Here are three reasons for the shift from domestic to _____ as given by the authors of the textbook, _____ Management--3rd Edition by Masaaki Kotabe and Kristiaan Helsen, 2004.

One of the product categories in which global competition has been easy to track is in U.S. automotive sales.

a. Digital marketing
b. Guerrilla Marketing
c. Global marketing
d. Diversity marketing

9. _____ refers to the production of some commodity or service, such as a television program, using a company's own funds, staff, or resources.

This is in contrast to production being outsourced (contracted out) to another company.

- Proprietary

a. Outsourcing
b. Intangible assets
c. ACNielsen
d. In-house

10. In economics, business, retail, and accounting, a _____ is the value of money that has been used up to produce something, and hence is not available for use anymore. In economics, a _____ is an alternative that is given up as a result of a decision. In business, the _____ may be one of acquisition, in which case the amount of money expended to acquire it is counted as _____.

a. Transaction cost
b. Cost
c. Variable cost
d. Fixed costs

Chapter 2. The Marketing Research Process

11. _____ is a contract between two parties, one being the employer and the other being the employee. An employee may be defined as: 'A person in the service of another under any contract of hire, express or implied, oral or written, where the employer has the power or right to control and direct the employee in the material details of how the work is to be performed.' Black's Law Dictionary page 471 (5th ed. 1979.)
    a. ACNielsen
    b. AMAX
    c. ADTECH
    d. Employment

12. _____ generally refers to a list of all planned expenses and revenues. It is a plan for saving and spending. A _____ is an important concept in microeconomics, which uses a _____ line to illustrate the trade-offs between two or more goods.
    a. 6-3-5 Brainwriting
    b. Power III
    c. 180SearchAssistant
    d. Budget

13. In economics and sociology, an _____ is any factor (financial or non-financial) that enables or motivates a particular course of action, or counts as a reason for preferring one choice to the alternatives. It is an expectation that encourages people to behave in a certain way. Since human beings are purposeful creatures, the study of _____ structures is central to the study of all economic activity (both in terms of individual decision-making and in terms of co-operation and competition within a larger institutional structure.)
    a. ACNielsen
    b. AMAX
    c. ADTECH
    d. Incentive

14. In statistics, an _____ is a term in a statistical model added when the effect of two or more variables is not simply additive. Such a term reflects that the effect of one variable depends on the values of one or more other variables.

Thus, for a response Y and two variables x_1 and x_2 an additive model would be:

$$Y = ax_1 + bx_2 + \text{error}$$

In contrast to this,

$$Y = ax_1 + bx_2 + c(x_1 \times x_2) + \text{error},$$

is an example of a model with an _____ between variables x_1 and x_2 ('error' refers to the random variable whose value by which y differs from the expected value of y.)

    a. Interaction
    b. ADTECH
    c. AMAX
    d. ACNielsen

15. The _____ is a statistical test used in inference, in which a given statistical hypothesis will be rejected when the value of the statistic is either sufficiently small or sufficiently large. The test is named after the 'tail' of data under the far left and far right of a bell-shaped normal data distribution, or bell curve. However, the terminology is extended to tests relating to distributions other than normal.

Chapter 2. The Marketing Research Process

a. Two-tailed test
c. Sampling error
b. Power III
d. Varimax rotation

16. _____ is a broad label that refers to any individuals or households that use goods and services generated within the economy. The concept of a _____ is used in different contexts, so that the usage and significance of the term may vary.

A _____ is a person who uses any product or service.

a. Consumer
c. 6-3-5 Brainwriting
b. Power III
d. 180SearchAssistant

17. _____, in strategic management and marketing, is the percentage or proportion of the total available market or market segment that is being serviced by a company. It can be expressed as a company's sales revenue (from that market) divided by the total sales revenue available in that market. It can also be expressed as a company's unit sales volume (in a market) divided by the total volume of units sold in that market.

a. Demand generation
c. Customer relationship management
b. Cyberdoc
d. Market share

18. _____, in marketing, consists of a consumer's commitment to repurchase the brand and can be demonstrated by repeated buying of a product or service or other positive behaviors such as word of mouth advocacy. True _____ implies that the consumer is willing, at least on occasion, to put aside their own desires in the interest of the brand. _____ has been proclaimed by some to be the ultimate goal of marketing.

a. Trade Symbols
c. Brand implementation
b. Brand awareness
d. Brand loyalty

19. _____ is one of the four Ps of the marketing mix. The other three aspects are product, promotion, and place. It is also a key variable in microeconomic price allocation theory.

a. Price
c. Competitor indexing
b. Relationship based pricing
d. Pricing

20. _____ is a measure of the strength of a brand, product, service relative to competitive offerings. There is often a geographic element to the competitive landscape. In defining _____, you must see to what extent a product, brand, or firm controls a product category in a given geographic area.

a. Market system
c. Productivity
b. Market dominance
d. Discretionary spending

21. In psychology, philosophy, and the cognitive sciences, _____ is the process of attaining awareness or understanding of sensory information. It is a task far more complex than was imagined in the 1950s and 1960s, when it was predicted that building perceiving machines would take about a decade, a goal which is still very far from fruition. The word _____ comes from the Latin words _____, percepio, meaning 'receiving, collecting, action of taking possession, apprehension with the mind or senses.'

_____ is one of the oldest fields in psychology.

a. 180SearchAssistant
c. Groupthink
b. Perception
d. Power III

22. The United States _____ is the government agency that is responsible for the United States Census. It also gathers other national demographic and economic data.
   a. Power III
   b. Census Bureau
   c. 6-3-5 Brainwriting
   d. 180SearchAssistant

23. _____ or _____ data refers to selected population characteristics as used in government, marketing or opinion research, or the _____ profiles used in such research. Note the distinction from the term 'demography' Commonly-used _____ include race, age, income, disabilities, mobility (in terms of travel time to work or number of vehicles available), educational attainment, home ownership, employment status, and even location.
   a. AStore
   b. African Americans
   c. Albert Einstein
   d. Demographic

24. _____ describes data and characteristics about the population or phenomenon being studied. _____ answers the questions who, what, where, when and how.

Although the data description is factual, accurate and systematic, the research cannot describe what caused a situation.
   a. Sampling error
   b. Two-tailed test
   c. Descriptive research
   d. Power III

25. _____ is a type of research conducted because a problem has not been clearly defined. _____ helps determine the best research design, data collection method and selection of subjects. Given its fundamental nature, _____ often concludes that a perceived problem does not actually exist.
   a. ACNielsen
   b. Intent scale translation
   c. IDDEA
   d. Exploratory research

26. _____ is a set of six steps which defines the tasks to be accomplished in conducting a marketing research study. These include problem definition, developing an approach to problem, research design formulation, field work, data preparation and analysis, and report generation and presentation.
   a. Simple random sampling
   b. Market analysis
   c. Preference-rank translation
   d. Marketing research process

27. In statistics, an _____ draws inferences about the effect of a treatment on subjects, where the assignment of subjects into a treated group versus a control group is outside the control of the investigator. This is in contrast with controlled experiments, such as randomized controlled trials, where each subject is randomly assigned to a treated group or a control group before the start of the treatment.

The assignment of treatments may be beyond the control of the investigator for a variety of reasons:

- A randomized experiment would violate ethical standards. Suppose one wanted to investigate the abortion-breast cancer hypothesis, which postulates a causal link between induced abortion and the incidence of breast cancer. In a hypothetical controlled experiment, one would start with a large subject pool of pregnant women and divide them randomly into a treatment group (receiving induced abortions) and a control group (bearing children), and then conduct regular cancer screenings for women from both groups. Needless to say, such an experiment would run counter to common ethical principles. (It would also suffer from various confounds and sources of bias, e.g., it would be impossible to conduct it as a blind experiment.) The published studies investigating the abortion-breast cancer hypothesis generally start with a group of women who already have received abortions. Membership in this 'treated' group is not controlled by the investigator: the group is formed after the 'treatment' has been assigned.

- The investigator may simply lack the requisite influence. Suppose a scientist wants to study the public health effects of a community-wide ban on smoking in public indoor areas.

a. ADTECH
b. Observational study
c. AMAX
d. ACNielsen

28. _____ in economics and business is the result of an exchange and from that trade we assign a numerical monetary value to a good, service or asset. If I trade 4 apples for an orange, the _____ of an orange is 4 - apples. Inversely, the _____ of an apple is 1/4 oranges.
a. Contribution margin-based pricing
b. Pricing
c. Discounts and allowances
d. Price

29. A number of different _____s are indicated below.

- Randomized controlled trial
  - Double-blind randomized trial
  - Single-blind randomized trial
  - Non-blind trial
- Nonrandomized trial (quasi-experiment)
  - Interrupted time series design (measures on a sample or a series of samples from the same population are obtained several times before and after a manipulated event or a naturally occurring event) - considered a type of quasi-experiment

- Cohort study
  - Prospective cohort
  - Retrospective cohort
  - Time series study
- Case-control study
  - Nested case-control study
- Cross-sectional study
  - Community survey (a type of cross-sectional study)

When choosing a _____, many factors must be taken into account. Different types of studies are subject to different types of bias. For example, recall bias is likely to occur in cross-sectional or case-control studies where subjects are asked to recall exposure to risk factors.

a. 180SearchAssistant
b. Longitudinal studies
c. Power III
d. Study design

30. _____s are used in open sentences. For instance, in the formula x + 1 = 5, x is a _____ which represents an 'unknown' number. _____s are often represented by letters of the Roman alphabet, or those of other alphabets, such as Greek, and use other special symbols.

a. Quantitative
b. Variable
c. Book of business
d. Personalization

31. _____ is the process of finding associated geographic coordinates (often expressed as latitude and longitude) from other geographic data, such as street addresses or the coordinates can be embedded into media such as digital photographs via geotagging.

Reverse _____ is the opposite: finding an associated textual location such as a street address, from geographic coordinates.

a. 180SearchAssistant
b. Geocoding
c. 6-3-5 Brainwriting
d. Power III

32. Sampling is the use of a subset of the population to represent the whole population. Probability sampling, or random sampling, is a sampling technique in which the probability of getting any particular sample may be calculated. _____ does not meet this criterion and should be used with caution.

a. Nonprobability sampling
b. Snowball sampling
c. Power III
d. Quota sampling

33. In probability theory and statistics, _____ indicates the strength and direction of a linear relationship between two random variables. That is in contrast with the usage of the term in colloquial speech, denoting any relationship, not necessarily linear. In general statistical usage, _____ or co-relation refers to the departure of two random variables from independence.

a. Correlation
b. Mean
c. Probability
d. Frequency distribution

34. _____ is one of the four elements of marketing mix. An organization or set of organizations (go-betweens) involved in the process of making a product or service available for use or consumption by a consumer or business user.

The other three parts of the marketing mix are product, pricing, and promotion.

a. Japan Advertising Photographers' Association
b. Comparison-Shopping agent
c. Better Living Through Chemistry
d. Distribution

35. In the mathematical discipline of graph theory a _____ or edge-independent set in a graph is a set of edges without common vertices. It may also be an entire graph consisting of edges without common vertices.

Given a graph G = (V,E), a _____ M in G is a set of pairwise non-adjacent edges; that is, no two edges share a common vertex.

   a. 6-3-5 Brainwriting   b. 180SearchAssistant
   c. Matching   d. Power III

36. _____ is that part of statistical practice concerned with the selection of individual observations intended to yield some knowledge about a population of concern, especially for the purposes of statistical inference. Each observation measures one or more properties (weight, location, etc.) of an observable entity enumerated to distinguish objects or individuals.
   a. Sports Marketing Group   b. Sampling
   c. AStore   d. Richard Buckminster 'Bucky' Fuller

37. _____ is a term used to describe a process of preparing and collecting data - for example as part of a process improvement or similar project.

_____ usually takes place early on in an improvement project, and is often formalised through a _____ Plan which often contains the following activity.

1. Pre collection activity - Agree goals, target data, definitions, methods
2. Collection - _____
3. Present Findings - usually involves some form of sorting analysis and/or presentation.

A formal _____ process is necessary as it ensures that data gathered is both defined and accurate and that subsequent decisions based on arguments embodied in the findings are valid . The process provides both a baseline from which to measure from and in certain cases a target on what to improve. Types of _____ 1-By mail questionnaires 2-By personal interview

- Six sigma
- Sampling (statistics)

   a. 180SearchAssistant   b. Data collection
   c. Power III   d. 6-3-5 Brainwriting

38. In marketing, _____ has come to mean the process by which marketers try to create an image or identity in the minds of their target market for its product, brand, or organization. It is the 'relative competitive comparison' their product occupies in a given market as perceived by the target market.

Re-_____ involves changing the identity of a product, relative to the identity of competing products, in the collective minds of the target market.

Chapter 2. The Marketing Research Process

a. Containerization
b. GE matrix
c. Moratorium
d. Positioning

39. _____ is a term for unprocessed data, it is also known as primary data. It is a relative term _____ can be input to a computer program or used in manual analysis procedures such as gathering statistics from a survey.
a. Shoppers Food ' Pharmacy
b. Raw data
c. Product manager
d. Chief marketing officer

40. _____ is the study of the Earth and its lands, features, inhabitants, and phenomena. A literal translation would be 'to describe or write about the Earth'. The first person to use the word '_____' was Eratosthenes .
a. 180SearchAssistant
b. Power III
c. 6-3-5 Brainwriting
d. Geography

41. _____ is systematic determination of merit, worth, and significance of something or someone using criteria against a set of standards. _____ often is used to characterize and appraise subjects of interest in a wide range of human enterprises, including the arts, criminal justice, foundations and non-profit organizations, government, health care, and other human services.

Depending on the topic of interest, there are professional groups which look to the quality and rigor of the _____ process.

a. ADTECH
b. AMAX
c. ACNielsen
d. Evaluation

42. _____ is a branch of philosophy which seeks to address questions about morality, such as how a moral outcome can be achieved in a specific situation (applied _____), how moral values should be determined (normative _____), what moral values people actually abide by (descriptive _____), what the fundamental semantic, ontological, and epistemic nature of _____ or morality is (meta-_____), and how moral capacity or moral agency develops and what its nature is (moral psychology.)

Socrates was one of the first Greek philosophers to encourage both scholars and the common citizen to turn their attention from the outside world to the condition of man. In this view, Knowledge having a bearing on human life was placed highest, all other knowledge being secondary.

a. ACNielsen
b. Ethics
c. AMAX
d. ADTECH

43. A _____ is a research instrument consisting of a series of questions and other prompts for the purpose of gathering information from respondents. Although they are often designed for statistical analysis of the responses, this is not always the case. The _____ was invented by Sir Francis Galton.
a. Market research
b. Mystery shoppers
c. Mystery shopping
d. Questionnaire

44. _____ is an advertisement in which a particular product specifically mentions a competitor by name for the express purpose of showing why the competitor is inferior to the product naming it.

This should not be confused with parody advertisements, where a fictional product is being advertised for the purpose of poking fun at the particular advertisement, nor should it be confused with the use of a coined brand name for the purpose of comparing the product without actually naming an actual competitor. ('Wikipedia tastes better and is less filling than the Encyclopedia Galactica.')

In the 1980s, during what has been referred to as the cola wars, soft-drink manufacturer Pepsi ran a series of advertisements where people, caught on hidden camera, in a blind taste test, chose Pepsi over rival Coca-Cola.

a. GL-70
b. Comparative advertising
c. Cost per conversion
d. Heavy-up

45. A supply chain is the system of organizations, people, technology, activities, information and resources involved in moving a product or service from _____ to customer. Supply chain activities transform natural resources, raw materials and components into a finished product that is delivered to the end customer. In sophisticated supply chain systems, used products may re-enter the supply chain at any point where residual value is recyclable.

a. Rebate
b. Product line extension
c. Bringin' Home the Oil
d. Supplier

46. _____ has been defined by the International Organization for Standardization (ISO) as 'ensuring that information is accessible only to those authorized to have access' and is one of the cornerstones of information security. _____ is one of the design goals for many cryptosystems, made possible in practice by the techniques of modern cryptography.

_____ also refers to an ethical principle associated with several professions (e.g., medicine, law, religion, professional psychology, and journalism.)

a. 180SearchAssistant
b. Power III
c. 6-3-5 Brainwriting
d. Confidentiality

47. A _____ is a plan of action designed to achieve a particular goal.

_____ is different from tactics. In military terms, tactics is concerned with the conduct of an engagement while _____ is concerned with how different engagements are linked.

a. Strategy
b. 6-3-5 Brainwriting
c. 180SearchAssistant
d. Power III

48. _____ is either an activity of a living being (such as a human), consisting of receiving knowledge of the outside world through the senses, or the recording of data using scientific instruments. The term may also refer to any datum collected during this activity.

The scientific method requires _____s of nature to formulate and test hypotheses.

a. ADTECH
c. ACNielsen
b. AMAX
d. Observation

Chapter 3. Types of Marketing Research

1. A _____ captures, stores, analyzes, manages, and presents data that is linked to location.

In the strictest sense, the term describes any information system that integrates, stores, edits, analyzes, shares, and displays geographic information. In a more generic sense, _____ applications are tools that allow users to create interactive queries (user created searches), analyze spatial information, edit data, maps, and present the results of all these operations.

   a. Power III
   b. 180SearchAssistant
   c. Geographic information system
   d. 6-3-5 Brainwriting

2. _____ is a type of research conducted because a problem has not been clearly defined. _____ helps determine the best research design, data collection method and selection of subjects. Given its fundamental nature, _____ often concludes that a perceived problem does not actually exist.
   a. Intent scale translation
   b. IDDEA
   c. ACNielsen
   d. Exploratory research

3. A supply chain is the system of organizations, people, technology, activities, information and resources involved in moving a product or service from _____ to customer. Supply chain activities transform natural resources, raw materials and components into a finished product that is delivered to the end customer. In sophisticated supply chain systems, used products may re-enter the supply chain at any point where residual value is recyclable.
   a. Product line extension
   b. Rebate
   c. Supplier
   d. Bringin' Home the Oil

4. _____ in economics and business is the result of an exchange and from that trade we assign a numerical monetary value to a good, service or asset. If I trade 4 apples for an orange, the _____ of an orange is 4 - apples. Inversely, the _____ of an apple is 1/4 oranges.
   a. Discounts and allowances
   b. Contribution margin-based pricing
   c. Pricing
   d. Price

5. _____ is defined by the American _____ Association as the activity, set of institutions, and processes for creating, communicating, delivering, and exchanging offerings that have value for customers, clients, partners, and society at large. The term developed from the original meaning which referred literally to going to market, as in shopping, or going to a market to sell goods or services.

_____ practice tends to be seen as a creative industry, which includes advertising, distribution and selling.

   a. Marketing myopia
   b. Marketing
   c. Product naming
   d. Customer acquisition management

6. Consumer market research is a form of applied sociology that concentrates on understanding the behaviours, whims and preferences, of consumers in a market-based economy, and aims to understand the effects and comparative success of marketing campaigns. The field of consumer _____ as a statistical science was pioneered by Arthur Nielsen with the founding of the ACNielsen Company in 1923.

Thus _____ is the systematic and objective identification, collection, analysis, and dissemination of information for the purpose of assisting management in decision making related to the identification and solution of problems and opportunities in marketing.

a. Logit analysis
b. Marketing research process
c. Focus group
d. Marketing research

7. An _____ is one type of focus group, and is a sub-set of online research methods.

A moderator invites prescreened, qualified respondents who represent the target of interest to log on to conferencing software at a pre-arranged time and to take part in an _____. Some researchers will offer incentives for participating but this raises a number of ethical questions.

a. Engagement
b. Intangibility
c. Online focus group
d. Automated surveys

8. A _____ is a form of qualitative research in which a group of people are asked about their attitude towards a product, service, concept, advertisement, idea, or packaging. Questions are asked in an interactive group setting where participants are free to talk with other group members.

Ernest Dichter originated the idea of having a 'group therapy' for products and this process is what became known as a _____.

a. Logit analysis
b. Marketing research process
c. Cross tabulation
d. Focus group

9. A _____ is a collection of symbols, experiences and associations connected with a product, a service, a person or any other artifact or entity.

_____s have become increasingly important components of culture and the economy, now being described as 'cultural accessories and personal philosophies'.

Some people distinguish the psychological aspect of a _____ from the experiential aspect.

a. Store brand
b. Brand equity
c. Brandable software
d. Brand

10. A _____ is typically the attributes one associates with a brand, how the brand owner wants the consumer to perceive the brand - and by extension the branded company, organization, product or service. The brand owner will seek to bridge the gap between the _____ and the brand identity.

a. Brand image
b. Brand loyalty
c. Status brand
d. Brand equity

11. In economics, an externality or spillover of an economic transaction is an impact on a party that is not directly involved in the transaction. In such a case, prices do not reflect the full costs or benefits in production or consumption of a product or service. A positive impact is called an _____ benefit, while a negative impact is called an _____ cost.

a. ADTECH
b. AMAX
c. ACNielsen
d. External

Chapter 3. Types of Marketing Research

12. _____ refer to a collection of facts usually collected as the result of experience, observation or experiment or a set of premises. This may consist of numbers, words particularly as measurements or observations of a set of variables. _____ are often viewed as a lowest level of abstraction from which information and knowledge are derived.
    a. Mean
    b. Sample size
    c. Data
    d. Pearson product-moment correlation coefficient

13. Combining Existing _____ Sources with New Primary Data Sources

Imagine that we could get hold of a good collection of surveys taken in earlier years, such as detailed studies about changes going on in this phase and hopefully additional studies in the years to come. Analyzing this data base over time could give us a good picture of what changes actually have taken place in the orientation of the population and of the extent to which new technical concepts did have an impact on subgroups of the population. Furthermore, data archives can help to prepare studies on change over time by monitoring what questions have been asked in earlier years and alerting principal investigators to important questions which should be repeated in planned research projects.

    a. Power III
    b. Secondary data
    c. 6-3-5 Brainwriting
    d. 180SearchAssistant

14. _____ can be regarded as an outcome of mental processes (cognitive process) leading to the selection of a course of action among several alternatives. Every _____ process produces a final choice. The output can be an action or an opinion of choice.
    a. Power III
    b. 180SearchAssistant
    c. 6-3-5 Brainwriting
    d. Decision making

15. _____ is a process of gathering, modeling, and transforming data with the goal of highlighting useful information, suggesting conclusions, and supporting decision making. _____ has multiple facets and approaches, encompassing diverse techniques under a variety of names, in different business, science, and social science domains.

Data mining is a particular _____ technique that focuses on modeling and knowledge discovery for predictive rather than purely descriptive purposes.

    a. 6-3-5 Brainwriting
    b. Data analysis
    c. Power III
    d. 180SearchAssistant

16. A _____ is a process that can allow an organization to concentrate its limited resources on the greatest opportunities to increase sales and achieve a sustainable competitive advantage. A _____ should be centered around the key concept that customer satisfaction is the main goal.

A _____ is most effective when it is an integral component of corporate strategy, defining how the organization will successfully engage customers, prospects, and competitors in the market arena.

    a. Cyberdoc
    b. Psychographic
    c. Societal marketing
    d. Marketing strategy

Chapter 3. Types of Marketing Research

17. _____ is either an activity of a living being (such as a human), consisting of receiving knowledge of the outside world through the senses, or the recording of data using scientific instruments. The term may also refer to any datum collected during this activity.

The scientific method requires _____s of nature to formulate and test hypotheses.

a. ADTECH
b. ACNielsen
c. Observation
d. AMAX

18. A _____ is a plan of action designed to achieve a particular goal.

_____ is different from tactics. In military terms, tactics is concerned with the conduct of an engagement while _____ is concerned with how different engagements are linked.

a. Strategy
b. 6-3-5 Brainwriting
c. Power III
d. 180SearchAssistant

19. _____ is a term developed by Eric von Hippel in 1986. His definition for _____ is:

1. _____s face needs that will be general in a marketplace - but face them months or years before the bulk of that marketplace encounters them, and
2. _____s are positioned to benefit significantly by obtaining a solution to those needs.

In other words: _____s are users of a product that currently experience needs still unknown to the public and who also benefit greatly if they obtain a solution to these needs.

The _____ Method is a market research tool that may be used by companies and / or individuals seeking to develop breakthrough products. _____ methodology was originally developed by Dr. Eric von Hippel of the Massachusetts Institute of Technology (MIT) and first described in the July 1986 issue of the Journal of Management Science.

a. 6-3-5 Brainwriting
b. 180SearchAssistant
c. Lead user
d. Power III

20. _____ describes data and characteristics about the population or phenomenon being studied. _____ answers the questions who, what, where, when and how.

Although the data description is factual, accurate and systematic, the research cannot describe what caused a situation.

a. Two-tailed test
b. Power III
c. Sampling error
d. Descriptive research

Chapter 3. Types of Marketing Research

21. _____ is a broad label that refers to any individuals or households that use goods and services generated within the economy. The concept of a _____ is used in different contexts, so that the usage and significance of the term may vary.

A _____ is a person who uses any product or service.

- a. 180SearchAssistant
- b. 6-3-5 Brainwriting
- c. Consumer
- d. Power III

22. _____ form a class of research methods that involve observation of some subset of a population of items all at the same time, in which, groups can be compared at different ages with respect of independent variables, such as IQ and memory. The fundamental difference between cross-sectional and longitudinal studies is that _____ take place at a single point in time and that a longitudinal study involves a series of measurements taken over a period of time. Both are a type of observational study.
- a. Power III
- b. Longitudinal studies
- c. Cross-sectional studies
- d. 180SearchAssistant

23. A longitudinal study is a correlational research study that involves repeated observations of the same items over long periods of time -- often many decades. It is a type of observational study. _____ are often used in psychology to study developmental trends across the life span.
- a. Power III
- b. 180SearchAssistant
- c. Study design
- d. Longitudinal studies

24. _____, in marketing, consists of a consumer's commitment to repurchase the brand and can be demonstrated by repeated buying of a product or service or other positive behaviors such as word of mouth advocacy. True _____ implies that the consumer is willing, at least on occasion, to put aside their own desires in the interest of the brand. _____ has been proclaimed by some to be the ultimate goal of marketing.
- a. Trade Symbols
- b. Brand awareness
- c. Brand implementation
- d. Brand loyalty

25. _____s are used in open sentences. For instance, in the formula x + 1 = 5, x is a _____ which represents an 'unknown' number. _____s are often represented by letters of the Roman alphabet, or those of other alphabets, such as Greek, and use other special symbols.
- a. Book of business
- b. Variable
- c. Quantitative
- d. Personalization

26. Advertising mail junk mail is the delivery of advertising material to recipients of postal mail. The delivery of advertising mail forms a large and growing service for many postal services, and _____ marketing forms a significant portion of the direct marketing industry. Some organizations attempt to help people opt-out of receiving advertising mail, in many cases motivated by a concern over its negative environmental impact.
- a. Direct mail
- b. Directory Harvest Attack
- c. Telemarketing
- d. Phishing

Chapter 3. Types of Marketing Research

27. _____ is a form of communication that typically attempts to persuade potential customers to purchase or to consume more of a particular brand of product or service. 'While now central to the contemporary global economy and the reproduction of global production networks, it is only quite recently that _____ has been more than a marginal influence on patterns of sales and production. The formation of modern _____ was intimately bound up with the emergence of new forms of monopoly capitalism around the end of the 19th and beginning of the 20th century as one element in corporate strategies to create, organize and where possible control markets, especially for mass produced consumer goods.

   a. ADTECH
   b. ACNielsen
   c. AMAX
   d. Advertising

28. _____ generally refers to a list of all planned expenses and revenues. It is a plan for saving and spending. A _____ is an important concept in microeconomics, which uses a _____ line to illustrate the trade-offs between two or more goods.

   a. Budget
   b. 6-3-5 Brainwriting
   c. Power III
   d. 180SearchAssistant

29. _____ is one of the four Ps of the marketing mix. The other three aspects are product, promotion, and place. It is also a key variable in microeconomic price allocation theory.

   a. Pricing
   b. Relationship based pricing
   c. Price
   d. Competitor indexing

30. _____, in strategic management and marketing, is the percentage or proportion of the total available market or market segment that is being serviced by a company. It can be expressed as a company's sales revenue (from that market) divided by the total sales revenue available in that market. It can also be expressed as a company's unit sales volume (in a market) divided by the total volume of units sold in that market.

   a. Customer relationship management
   b. Cyberdoc
   c. Market share
   d. Demand generation

31. _____ is an advertisement in which a particular product specifically mentions a competitor by name for the express purpose of showing why the competitor is inferior to the product naming it.

This should not be confused with parody advertisements, where a fictional product is being advertised for the purpose of poking fun at the particular advertisement, nor should it be confused with the use of a coined brand name for the purpose of comparing the product without actually naming an actual competitor. ('Wikipedia tastes better and is less filling than the Encyclopedia Galactica.')

In the 1980s, during what has been referred to as the cola wars, soft-drink manufacturer Pepsi ran a series of advertisements where people, caught on hidden camera, in a blind taste test, chose Pepsi over rival Coca-Cola.

   a. Heavy-up
   b. GL-70
   c. Cost per conversion
   d. Comparative advertising

Chapter 4. Secondary Data

1. A _____ is a structured collection of records or data that is stored in a computer system. The structure is achieved by organizing the data according to a _____ model. The model in most common use today is the relational model.
   - a. 6-3-5 Brainwriting
   - b. Power III
   - c. 180SearchAssistant
   - d. Database

2. In economics, an externality or spillover of an economic transaction is an impact on a party that is not directly involved in the transaction. In such a case, prices do not reflect the full costs or benefits in production or consumption of a product or service. A positive impact is called an _____ benefit, while a negative impact is called an _____ cost.
   - a. AMAX
   - b. External
   - c. ACNielsen
   - d. ADTECH

3. _____ refer to a collection of facts usually collected as the result of experience, observation or experiment or a set of premises. This may consist of numbers, words particularly as measurements or observations of a set of variables. _____ are often viewed as a lowest level of abstraction from which information and knowledge are derived.
   - a. Mean
   - b. Sample size
   - c. Pearson product-moment correlation coefficient
   - d. Data

4. Combining Existing _____ Sources with New Primary Data Sources

Imagine that we could get hold of a good collection of surveys taken in earlier years, such as detailed studies about changes going on in this phase and hopefully additional studies in the years to come. Analyzing this data base over time could give us a good picture of what changes actually have taken place in the orientation of the population and of the extent to which new technical concepts did have an impact on subgroups of the population. Furthermore, data archives can help to prepare studies on change over time by monitoring what questions have been asked in earlier years and alerting principal investigators to important questions which should be repeated in planned research projects.

   - a. 6-3-5 Brainwriting
   - b. Secondary data
   - c. Power III
   - d. 180SearchAssistant

5. _____ is a term used to describe a process of preparing and collecting data - for example as part of a process improvement or similar project.

_____ usually takes place early on in an improvement project, and is often formalised through a _____ Plan which often contains the following activity.

   1. Pre collection activity - Agree goals, target data, definitions, methods
   2. Collection - _____
   3. Present Findings - usually involves some form of sorting analysis and/or presentation.

A formal _____ process is necessary as it ensures that data gathered is both defined and accurate and that subsequent decisions based on arguments embodied in the findings are valid . The process provides both a baseline from which to measure from and in certain cases a target on what to improve. Types of _____ 1-By mail questionnaires 2-By personal interview

- Six sigma
- Sampling (statistics)

a. 6-3-5 Brainwriting
c. Power III
b. 180SearchAssistant
d. Data collection

6. A supply chain is the system of organizations, people, technology, activities, information and resources involved in moving a product or service from _____ to customer. Supply chain activities transform natural resources, raw materials and components into a finished product that is delivered to the end customer. In sophisticated supply chain systems, used products may re-enter the supply chain at any point where residual value is recyclable.

a. Supplier
c. Bringin' Home the Oil
b. Product line extension
d. Rebate

7. _____s are used in open sentences. For instance, in the formula x + 1 = 5, x is a _____ which represents an 'unknown' number. _____s are often represented by letters of the Roman alphabet, or those of other alphabets, such as Greek, and use other special symbols.

a. Book of business
c. Variable
b. Personalization
d. Quantitative

8. _____ is defined by the American _____ Association as the activity, set of institutions, and processes for creating, communicating, delivering, and exchanging offerings that have value for customers, clients, partners, and society at large. The term developed from the original meaning which referred literally to going to market, as in shopping, or going to a market to sell goods or services.

_____ practice tends to be seen as a creative industry, which includes advertising, distribution and selling.

a. Customer acquisition management
c. Product naming
b. Marketing myopia
d. Marketing

9. Consumer market research is a form of applied sociology that concentrates on understanding the behaviours, whims and preferences, of consumers in a market-based economy, and aims to understand the effects and comparative success of marketing campaigns. The field of consumer _____ as a statistical science was pioneered by Arthur Nielsen with the founding of the ACNielsen Company in 1923 .

Thus _____ is the systematic and objective identification, collection, analysis, and dissemination of information for the purpose of assisting management in decision making related to the identification and solution of problems and opportunities in marketing.

a. Marketing research process
b. Marketing research
c. Focus group
d. Logit analysis

10. The United States _____ is the government agency that is responsible for the United States Census. It also gathers other national demographic and economic data.
   a. 6-3-5 Brainwriting
   b. Power III
   c. Census Bureau
   d. 180SearchAssistant

11. In statistics, an _____ draws inferences about the effect of a treatment on subjects, where the assignment of subjects into a treated group versus a control group is outside the control of the investigator. This is in contrast with controlled experiments, such as randomized controlled trials, where each subject is randomly assigned to a treated group or a control group before the start of the treatment.

The assignment of treatments may be beyond the control of the investigator for a variety of reasons:

- A randomized experiment would violate ethical standards. Suppose one wanted to investigate the abortion-breast cancer hypothesis, which postulates a causal link between induced abortion and the incidence of breast cancer. In a hypothetical controlled experiment, one would start with a large subject pool of pregnant women and divide them randomly into a treatment group (receiving induced abortions) and a control group (bearing children), and then conduct regular cancer screenings for women from both groups. Needless to say, such an experiment would run counter to common ethical principles. (It would also suffer from various confounds and sources of bias, e.g., it would be impossible to conduct it as a blind experiment.) The published studies investigating the abortion-breast cancer hypothesis generally start with a group of women who already have received abortions. Membership in this 'treated' group is not controlled by the investigator: the group is formed after the 'treatment' has been assigned.

- The investigator may simply lack the requisite influence. Suppose a scientist wants to study the public health effects of a community-wide ban on smoking in public indoor areas.

   a. ADTECH
   b. Observational study
   c. ACNielsen
   d. AMAX

12. Electronic commerce, commonly known as _____ or eCommerce, consists of the buying and selling of products or services over electronic systems such as the Internet and other computer networks. The amount of trade conducted electronically has grown extraordinarily with wide-spread Internet usage. A wide variety of commerce is conducted in this way, spurring and drawing on innovations in electronic funds transfer, supply chain management, Internet marketing, online transaction processing, electronic data interchange (EDI), inventory management systems, and automated data collection systems.
   a. ACNielsen
   b. AMAX
   c. E-commerce
   d. ADTECH

13. _____ is a mathematical science pertaining to the collection, analysis, interpretation or explanation, and presentation of data. It also provides tools for prediction and forecasting based on data. It is applicable to a wide variety of academic disciplines, from the natural and social sciences to the humanities, government and business.

Chapter 4. Secondary Data

a. Null hypothesis
c. Median
b. Statistics
d. Type I error

14. The Oxford University Press defines _____ as 'marketing on a worldwide scale reconciling or taking commercial advantage of global operational differences, similarities and opportunities in order to meet global objectives.' Oxford University Press' Glossary of Marketing Terms.

Here are three reasons for the shift from domestic to _____ as given by the authors of the textbook, _____ Management--3rd Edition by Masaaki Kotabe and Kristiaan Helsen, 2004.

One of the product categories in which global competition has been easy to track is in U.S. automotive sales.

a. Diversity marketing
c. Digital marketing
b. Guerrilla Marketing
d. Global marketing

15. _____ refers to the production of some commodity or service, such as a television program, using a company's own funds, staff, or resources.

This is in contrast to production being outsourced (contracted out) to another company.

- Proprietary

a. Intangible assets
c. ACNielsen
b. Outsourcing
d. In-house

16. _____ is a measure of the strength of a brand, product, service relative to competitive offerings. There is often a geographic element to the competitive landscape. In defining _____, you must see to what extent a product, brand, or firm controls a product category in a given geographic area.
a. Market system
c. Market dominance
b. Productivity
d. Discretionary spending

17. _____ is a term for unprocessed data, it is also known as primary data. It is a relative term _____ can be input to a computer program or used in manual analysis procedures such as gathering statistics from a survey.
a. Shoppers Food ' Pharmacy
c. Product manager
b. Raw data
d. Chief marketing officer

18. _____ was originally coined by Austrian psychologist Alfred Adler in 1929. The current broader sense of the word dates from 1961.

In sociology, a _____ is the way a person lives.

a. 6-3-5 Brainwriting
c. 180SearchAssistant
b. Power III
d. Lifestyle

19. A _____ attribute is one that exists in a range of magnitudes, and can therefore be measured. Measurements of any particular _____ property are expressed as a specific quantity, referred to as a unit, multiplied by a number. Examples of physical quantities are distance, mass, and time.
   a. Lifestyle city
   b. Quantitative
   c. BeyondROI
   d. Dolly Dimples

20. _____ is a broad label that refers to any individuals or households that use goods and services generated within the economy. The concept of a _____ is used in different contexts, so that the usage and significance of the term may vary.

A _____ is a person who uses any product or service.

   a. 6-3-5 Brainwriting
   b. Power III
   c. 180SearchAssistant
   d. Consumer

21. Competitiveness is a comparative concept of the ability and performance of a firm, sub-sector or country to sell and supply goods and/or services in a given market. Although widely used in economics and business management, the usefulness of the concept, particularly in the context of national competitiveness, is vigorously disputed by economists, such as Paul Krugman .

The term may also be applied to markets, where it is used to refer to the extent to which the market structure may be regarded as perfectly _____.

   a. Free trade zone
   b. Customs union
   c. Geographical pricing
   d. Competitive

22. An _____ is a special-purpose computer system designed to perform one or a few dedicated functions, often with real-time computing constraints. It is usually embedded as part of a complete device including hardware and mechanical parts. In contrast, a general-purpose computer, such as a personal computer, can do many different tasks depending on programming.
   a. AMAX
   b. ACNielsen
   c. ADTECH
   d. Embedded system

23. A _____ is a written document that details the necessary actions to achieve one or more marketing objectives. It can be for a product or service, a brand, or a product line. _____s cover between one and five years.
   a. Marketing plan
   b. Prosumer
   c. Disruptive technology
   d. Marketing strategy

24. _____ or _____ data refers to selected population characteristics as used in government, marketing or opinion research, or the _____ profiles used in such research. Note the distinction from the term 'demography' Commonly-used _____ include race, age, income, disabilities, mobility (in terms of travel time to work or number of vehicles available), educational attainment, home ownership, employment status, and even location.
   a. African Americans
   b. Demographic
   c. AStore
   d. Albert Einstein

Chapter 4. Secondary Data

25. _____ is a term used in business for a short document that summarises a longer report, proposal or group of related reports in such a way that readers can rapidly become acquainted with a large body of material without having to read it all. It will usually contain a brief statement of the problem or proposal covered in the major document(s), background information, concise analysis and main conclusions. It is intended as an aid to decision making by business managers.
   a. ACNielsen
   b. AMAX
   c. ADTECH
   d. Executive summary

26. A _____ is a commercial building for storage of goods. _____s are used by manufacturers, importers, exporters, wholesalers, transport businesses, customs, etc. They are usually large plain buildings in industrial areas of cities and towns.
   a. 6-3-5 Brainwriting
   b. 180SearchAssistant
   c. Power III
   d. Warehouse

27. _____ generally refers to a list of all planned expenses and revenues. It is a plan for saving and spending. A _____ is an important concept in microeconomics, which uses a _____ line to illustrate the trade-offs between two or more goods.
   a. Budget
   b. Power III
   c. 6-3-5 Brainwriting
   d. 180SearchAssistant

28. _____ involves disseminating information about a product, product line, brand, or company. It is one of the four key aspects of the marketing mix. (The other three elements are product marketing, pricing, and distribution). P>_____ is generally sub-divided into two parts:

   - Above the line _____: Promotion in the media (e.g. TV, radio, newspapers, Internet and Mobile Phones) in which the advertiser pays an advertising agency to place the ad
   - Below the line _____: All other _____. Much of this is intended to be subtle enough for the consumer to be unaware that _____ is taking place. E.g. sponsorship, product placement, endorsements, sales _____, merchandising, direct mail, personal selling, public relations, trade shows

   a. Cashmere Agency
   b. Promotion
   c. Davie Brown Index
   d. Bottling lines

29. '_____' is a class of statistical techniques that can be applied to data that exhibit 'natural' groupings. _____ sorts through the raw data and groups them into clusters. A cluster is a group of relatively homogeneous cases or observations.
   a. Cluster analysis
   b. 180SearchAssistant
   c. Power III
   d. Structure mining

30. _____ is a form of communication that typically attempts to persuade potential customers to purchase or to consume more of a particular brand of product or service. 'While now central to the contemporary global economy and the reproduction of global production networks, it is only quite recently that _____ has been more than a marginal influence on patterns of sales and production. The formation of modern _____ was intimately bound up with the emergence of new forms of monopoly capitalism around the end of the 19th and beginning of the 20th century as one element in corporate strategies to create, organize and where possible control markets, especially for mass produced consumer goods.

a. Advertising
b. AMAX
c. ACNielsen
d. ADTECH

31. A _____ is a subgroup of people or organizations sharing one or more characteristics that cause them to have similar product and/or service needs. A true _____ meets all of the following criteria: it is distinct from other segments (different segments have different needs), it is homogeneous within the segment (exhibits common needs); it responds similarly to a market stimulus, and it can be reached by a market intervention. The term is also used when consumers with identical product and/or service needs are divided up into groups so they can be charged different amounts.
   a. Commercial planning
   b. Customer insight
   c. Production orientation
   d. Market segment

32. _____ is the study of the Earth and its lands, features, inhabitants, and phenomena. A literal translation would be 'to describe or write about the Earth'. The first person to use the word '_____' was Eratosthenes.
   a. 6-3-5 Brainwriting
   b. Power III
   c. 180SearchAssistant
   d. Geography

33. _____ is that part of statistical practice concerned with the selection of individual observations intended to yield some knowledge about a population of concern, especially for the purposes of statistical inference. Each observation measures one or more properties (weight, location, etc.) of an observable entity enumerated to distinguish objects or individuals.
   a. Richard Buckminster 'Bucky' Fuller
   b. Sports Marketing Group
   c. AStore
   d. Sampling

Chapter 5. Using Geographic Information Systems for Marketing Research

1. _____ or _____ data refers to selected population characteristics as used in government, marketing or opinion research, or the _____ profiles used in such research. Note the distinction from the term 'demography' Commonly-used _____ include race, age, income, disabilities, mobility (in terms of travel time to work or number of vehicles available), educational attainment, home ownership, employment status, and even location.
   a. AStore
   b. African Americans
   c. Albert Einstein
   d. Demographic

2. In economics, an externality or spillover of an economic transaction is an impact on a party that is not directly involved in the transaction. In such a case, prices do not reflect the full costs or benefits in production or consumption of a product or service. A positive impact is called an _____ benefit, while a negative impact is called an _____ cost.
   a. ACNielsen
   b. ADTECH
   c. External
   d. AMAX

3. _____ is the study of the Earth and its lands, features, inhabitants, and phenomena. A literal translation would be 'to describe or write about the Earth'. The first person to use the word '_____' was Eratosthenes.
   a. Power III
   b. 180SearchAssistant
   c. 6-3-5 Brainwriting
   d. Geography

4. A _____ captures, stores, analyzes, manages, and presents data that is linked to location.

In the strictest sense, the term describes any information system that integrates, stores, edits, analyzes, shares, and displays geographic information. In a more generic sense, _____ applications are tools that allow users to create interactive queries (user created searches), analyze spatial information, edit data, maps, and present the results of all these operations.

   a. Power III
   b. 6-3-5 Brainwriting
   c. 180SearchAssistant
   d. Geographic information system

5. The Oxford University Press defines _____ as 'marketing on a worldwide scale reconciling or taking commercial advantage of global operational differences, similarities and opportunities in order to meet global objectives.' Oxford University Press' Glossary of Marketing Terms.

Here are three reasons for the shift from domestic to _____ as given by the authors of the textbook, _____ Management--3rd Edition by Masaaki Kotabe and Kristiaan Helsen, 2004.

One of the product categories in which global competition has been easy to track is in U.S. automotive sales.

   a. Global marketing
   b. Guerrilla Marketing
   c. Digital marketing
   d. Diversity marketing

6. _____ refers to the production of some commodity or service, such as a television program, using a company's own funds, staff, or resources.

Chapter 5. Using Geographic Information Systems for Marketing Research

This is in contrast to production being outsourced (contracted out) to another company.

- Proprietary

a. Intangible assets
c. ACNielsen
b. Outsourcing
d. In-house

7. In probability theory and statistics, _____ indicates the strength and direction of a linear relationship between two random variables. That is in contrast with the usage of the term in colloquial speech, denoting any relationship, not necessarily linear. In general statistical usage, _____ or co-relation refers to the departure of two random variables from independence.

a. Mean
c. Probability
b. Frequency distribution
d. Correlation

8. _____ refer to a collection of facts usually collected as the result of experience, observation or experiment or a set of premises. This may consist of numbers, words particularly as measurements or observations of a set of variables. _____ are often viewed as a lowest level of abstraction from which information and knowledge are derived.

a. Pearson product-moment correlation coefficient
c. Mean
b. Sample size
d. Data

9. _____ is defined by the American _____ Association as the activity, set of institutions, and processes for creating, communicating, delivering, and exchanging offerings that have value for customers, clients, partners, and society at large. The term developed from the original meaning which referred literally to going to market, as in shopping, or going to a market to sell goods or services.

_____ practice tends to be seen as a creative industry, which includes advertising, distribution and selling.

a. Marketing myopia
c. Customer acquisition management
b. Product naming
d. Marketing

10. Consumer market research is a form of applied sociology that concentrates on understanding the behaviours, whims and preferences, of consumers in a market-based economy, and aims to understand the effects and comparative success of marketing campaigns. The field of consumer _____ as a statistical science was pioneered by Arthur Nielsen with the founding of the ACNielsen Company in 1923.

Thus _____ is the systematic and objective identification, collection, analysis, and dissemination of information for the purpose of assisting management in decision making related to the identification and solution of problems and opportunities in marketing.

a. Focus group
c. Marketing research process
b. Logit analysis
d. Marketing research

Chapter 5. Using Geographic Information Systems for Marketing Research

11. _____ is a form of communication that typically attempts to persuade potential customers to purchase or to consume more of a particular brand of product or service. 'While now central to the contemporary global economy and the reproduction of global production networks, it is only quite recently that _____ has been more than a marginal influence on patterns of sales and production. The formation of modern _____ was intimately bound up with the emergence of new forms of monopoly capitalism around the end of the 19th and beginning of the 20th century as one element in corporate strategies to create, organize and where possible control markets, especially for mass produced consumer goods.

   a. Advertising
   b. AMAX
   c. ACNielsen
   d. ADTECH

12. _____ is the process of finding associated geographic coordinates (often expressed as latitude and longitude) from other geographic data, such as street addresses or the coordinates can be embedded into media such as digital photographs via geotagging.

    Reverse _____ is the opposite: finding an associated textual location such as a street address, from geographic coordinates.

    a. 180SearchAssistant
    b. 6-3-5 Brainwriting
    c. Power III
    d. Geocoding

13. _____ is a list for goods and materials held available in stock by a business. It is also used for a list of the contents of a household and for a list for testamentary purposes of the possessions of someone who has died. In accounting _____ is considered an asset.

    a. Ending Inventory
    b. ADTECH
    c. ACNielsen
    d. Inventory

14. The _____ is an equation that equals the cost of goods sold divided by the average inventory. Average inventory equals beginning inventory plus ending inventory divided by 2.

    The formula for _____:

    $$\text{Inventory Turnover} = \frac{\text{Cost of Goods Sold}}{\text{Average Inventory}}$$

    The formula for average inventory:

    $$\text{Average Inventory} = \frac{\text{Beginning inventory} + \text{Ending inventory}}{2}$$

    A low turnover rate may point to overstocking, obsolescence, or deficiencies in the product line or marketing effort.

    a. Inventory turnover
    b. AMAX
    c. ACNielsen
    d. ADTECH

Chapter 5. Using Geographic Information Systems for Marketing Research

15. _____ generally refers to a list of all planned expenses and revenues. It is a plan for saving and spending. A _____ is an important concept in microeconomics, which uses a _____ line to illustrate the trade-offs between two or more goods.

   a. 180SearchAssistant
   b. Budget
   c. 6-3-5 Brainwriting
   d. Power III

16. _____ refers to the methods, practices and operations conducted to promote and sustain certain categories of commercial activity. The term is understood to have different specific meanings depending on the context. Merchandise is a sale goods at a store

In marketing, one of the definitions of _____ is the practice in which the brand or image from one product or service is used to sell another.

   a. Word of mouth
   b. Marketing communication
   c. Merchandising
   d. New Media Strategies

17. _____ is a broad label that refers to any individuals or households that use goods and services generated within the economy. The concept of a _____ is used in different contexts, so that the usage and significance of the term may vary.

A _____ is a person who uses any product or service.

   a. 180SearchAssistant
   b. 6-3-5 Brainwriting
   c. Power III
   d. Consumer

18. In economics, _____ is the desire to own something and the ability to pay for it. The term _____ signifies the ability or the willingness to buy a particular commodity at a given point of time.

   a. Discretionary spending
   b. Market dominance
   c. Market system
   d. Demand

19. _____ is one of the four Ps of the marketing mix. The other three aspects are product, promotion, and place. It is also a key variable in microeconomic price allocation theory.

   a. Pricing
   b. Competitor indexing
   c. Price
   d. Relationship based pricing

20. In statistics, _____ is used for two things;

   - to construct a simple formula that will predict what value will occur for a quantity of interest when other related variables take given values.
   - to allow a test to be made of whether a given variable does have an effect on a quantity of interest in situations where there may be many related variables.

In both cases, several sets of outcomes are available for the quantity of interest together with the related variables.

Chapter 5. Using Geographic Information Systems for Marketing Research 39

_____ is a form of regression analysis in which the relationship between one or more independent variables and another variable, called the dependent variable, is modelled by a least squares function, called a _____ equation. This function is a linear combination of one or more model parameters, called regression coefficients. A _____ equation with one independent variable represents a straight line when the predicted value (i.e. the dependant variable from the regression equation) is plotted against the independent variable: this is called a simple _____.

a. Heteroskedastic
b. Sample size
c. Descriptive statistics
d. Linear regression

21. _____ refers to optimizing delivering ads according to the position of the recipient (client, user.) It is used in Geo (marketing.) Local search (Internet) often fuels uses optimization for targeting the advertising.
a. Bumvertising
b. Puffery
c. Jingle
d. Local advertising

22. A _____ is a plan of action designed to achieve a particular goal.

_____ is different from tactics. In military terms, tactics is concerned with the conduct of an engagement while _____ is concerned with how different engagements are linked.

a. 180SearchAssistant
b. Power III
c. 6-3-5 Brainwriting
d. Strategy

23. The United States _____ is the government agency that is responsible for the United States Census. It also gathers other national demographic and economic data.
a. Power III
b. 180SearchAssistant
c. 6-3-5 Brainwriting
d. Census Bureau

24. In statistics, an _____ draws inferences about the effect of a treatment on subjects, where the assignment of subjects into a treated group versus a control group is outside the control of the investigator. This is in contrast with controlled experiments, such as randomized controlled trials, where each subject is randomly assigned to a treated group or a control group before the start of the treatment.

The assignment of treatments may be beyond the control of the investigator for a variety of reasons:

- A randomized experiment would violate ethical standards. Suppose one wanted to investigate the abortion-breast cancer hypothesis, which postulates a causal link between induced abortion and the incidence of breast cancer. In a hypothetical controlled experiment, one would start with a large subject pool of pregnant women and divide them randomly into a treatment group (receiving induced abortions) and a control group (bearing children), and then conduct regular cancer screenings for women from both groups. Needless to say, such an experiment would run counter to common ethical principles. (It would also suffer from various confounds and sources of bias, e.g., it would be impossible to conduct it as a blind experiment.) The published studies investigating the abortion-breast cancer hypothesis generally start with a group of women who already have received abortions. Membership in this 'treated' group is not controlled by the investigator: the group is formed after the 'treatment' has been assigned.

- The investigator may simply lack the requisite influence. Suppose a scientist wants to study the public health effects of a community-wide ban on smoking in public indoor areas.

a. ADTECH
b. ACNielsen
c. AMAX
d. Observational study

25. _____ is a statistical method used to describe variability among observed variables in terms of fewer unobserved variables called factors. The observed variables are modeled as linear combinations of the factors, plus 'error' terms. The information gained about the interdependencies can be used later to reduce the set of variables in a dataset.
a. Likert scale
b. Semantic differential
c. Power III
d. Factor analysis

26. In marketing and strategy, _____ refers to a reduction in the sales volume, sales revenue, or market share of one product as a result of the introduction of a new product by the same producer.

For example, if Coca Cola were to introduce a similar product (say, Diet Coke or Cherry Coke), this new product could take some of the sales away from the original Coke. _____ is a key consideration in product portfolio analysis.

a. Marketing
b. Business-to-consumer
c. Co-marketing
d. Cannibalization

Chapter 6. Primary-Data Collection

1. _____ is one of the four Ps of the marketing mix. The other three aspects are product, promotion, and place. It is also a key variable in microeconomic price allocation theory.
   a. Competitor indexing
   b. Pricing
   c. Relationship based pricing
   d. Price

2. _____ is a term for unprocessed data, it is also known as primary data. It is a relative term _____ can be input to a computer program or used in manual analysis procedures such as gathering statistics from a survey.
   a. Chief marketing officer
   b. Shoppers Food ' Pharmacy
   c. Raw data
   d. Product manager

3. _____ refer to a collection of facts usually collected as the result of experience, observation or experiment or a set of premises. This may consist of numbers, words particularly as measurements or observations of a set of variables. _____ are often viewed as a lowest level of abstraction from which information and knowledge are derived.
   a. Mean
   b. Pearson product-moment correlation coefficient
   c. Sample size
   d. Data

4. _____ is a term used to describe a process of preparing and collecting data - for example as part of a process improvement or similar project.

   _____ usually takes place early on in an improvement project, and is often formalised through a _____ Plan which often contains the following activity.

   1. Pre collection activity - Agree goals, target data, definitions, methods
   2. Collection - _____
   3. Present Findings - usually involves some form of sorting analysis and/or presentation.

   A formal _____ process is necessary as it ensures that data gathered is both defined and accurate and that subsequent decisions based on arguments embodied in the findings are valid . The process provides both a baseline from which to measure from and in certain cases a target on what to improve. Types of _____ 1-By mail questionnaires 2-By personal interview

   - Six sigma
   - Sampling (statistics)

   a. Power III
   b. 180SearchAssistant
   c. Data collection
   d. 6-3-5 Brainwriting

5. The United States _____ is the government agency that is responsible for the United States Census. It also gathers other national demographic and economic data.
   a. 180SearchAssistant
   b. Census Bureau
   c. Power III
   d. 6-3-5 Brainwriting

6. In statistics, an _____ draws inferences about the effect of a treatment on subjects, where the assignment of subjects into a treated group versus a control group is outside the control of the investigator. This is in contrast with controlled experiments, such as randomized controlled trials, where each subject is randomly assigned to a treated group or a control group before the start of the treatment.

The assignment of treatments may be beyond the control of the investigator for a variety of reasons:

- A randomized experiment would violate ethical standards. Suppose one wanted to investigate the abortion-breast cancer hypothesis, which postulates a causal link between induced abortion and the incidence of breast cancer. In a hypothetical controlled experiment, one would start with a large subject pool of pregnant women and divide them randomly into a treatment group (receiving induced abortions) and a control group (bearing children), and then conduct regular cancer screenings for women from both groups. Needless to say, such an experiment would run counter to common ethical principles. (It would also suffer from various confounds and sources of bias, e.g., it would be impossible to conduct it as a blind experiment.) The published studies investigating the abortion-breast cancer hypothesis generally start with a group of women who already have received abortions. Membership in this 'treated' group is not controlled by the investigator: the group is formed after the 'treatment' has been assigned.

- The investigator may simply lack the requisite influence. Suppose a scientist wants to study the public health effects of a community-wide ban on smoking in public indoor areas.

a. AMAX
b. ACNielsen
c. Observational study
d. ADTECH

7. _____ involves disseminating information about a product, product line, brand, or company. It is one of the four key aspects of the marketing mix. (The other three elements are product marketing, pricing, and distribution). P>_____ is generally sub-divided into two parts:

- Above the line _____: Promotion in the media (e.g. TV, radio, newspapers, Internet and Mobile Phones) in which the advertiser pays an advertising agency to place the ad
- Below the line _____: All other _____. Much of this is intended to be subtle enough for the consumer to be unaware that _____ is taking place. E.g. sponsorship, product placement, endorsements, sales _____, merchandising, direct mail, personal selling, public relations, trade shows

a. Promotion
b. Cashmere Agency
c. Bottling lines
d. Davie Brown Index

8. A _____ is a research instrument consisting of a series of questions and other prompts for the purpose of gathering information from respondents. Although they are often designed for statistical analysis of the responses, this is not always the case. The _____ was invented by Sir Francis Galton.
a. Mystery shoppers
b. Questionnaire
c. Market research
d. Mystery shopping

9. _____ describes data and characteristics about the population or phenomenon being studied. _____ answers the questions who, what, where, when and how.

Although the data description is factual, accurate and systematic, the research cannot describe what caused a situation.

a. Power III
b. Sampling error
c. Two-tailed test
d. Descriptive research

10. _____ is a type of research conducted because a problem has not been clearly defined. _____ helps determine the best research design, data collection method and selection of subjects. Given its fundamental nature, _____ often concludes that a perceived problem does not actually exist.
a. IDDEA
b. Intent scale translation
c. ACNielsen
d. Exploratory research

11. _____ or _____ data refers to selected population characteristics as used in government, marketing or opinion research, or the _____ profiles used in such research. Note the distinction from the term 'demography' Commonly-used _____ include race, age, income, disabilities, mobility (in terms of travel time to work or number of vehicles available), educational attainment, home ownership, employment status, and even location.
a. Demographic
b. AStore
c. African Americans
d. Albert Einstein

12. _____ is defined by the American _____ Association as the activity, set of institutions, and processes for creating, communicating, delivering, and exchanging offerings that have value for customers, clients, partners, and society at large. The term developed from the original meaning which referred literally to going to market, as in shopping, or going to a market to sell goods or services.

_____ practice tends to be seen as a creative industry, which includes advertising, distribution and selling.

a. Marketing myopia
b. Customer acquisition management
c. Marketing
d. Product naming

13. Consumer market research is a form of applied sociology that concentrates on understanding the behaviours, whims and preferences, of consumers in a market-based economy, and aims to understand the effects and comparative success of marketing campaigns. The field of consumer _____ as a statistical science was pioneered by Arthur Nielsen with the founding of the ACNielsen Company in 1923.

Thus _____ is the systematic and objective identification, collection, analysis, and dissemination of information for the purpose of assisting management in decision making related to the identification and solution of problems and opportunities in marketing.

a. Logit analysis
b. Marketing research process
c. Focus group
d. Marketing research

14. _____ consists of the sale of goods or merchandise from a fixed location, such as a department store or kiosk in small or individual lots for direct consumption by the purchaser. _____ may include subordinated services, such as delivery. Purchasers may be individuals or businesses.
a. Charity shop
b. Warehouse store
c. Retailing
d. Thrifting

15. _____ is anything that is intended to save time, energy or frustration. A _____ store at a petrol station, for example, sells items that have nothing to do with gasoline/petrol, but it saves the consumer from having to go to a grocery store. '_____' is a very relative term and its meaning tends to change over time.
   a. Marketing buzz
   b. Demographic profile
   c. Convenience
   d. MaxDiff

16. _____ is either an activity of a living being (such as a human), consisting of receiving knowledge of the outside world through the senses, or the recording of data using scientific instruments. The term may also refer to any datum collected during this activity.

The scientific method requires _____s of nature to formulate and test hypotheses.

   a. ADTECH
   b. ACNielsen
   c. AMAX
   d. Observation

17. An _____ is a special-purpose computer system designed to perform one or a few dedicated functions, often with real-time computing constraints. It is usually embedded as part of a complete device including hardware and mechanical parts. In contrast, a general-purpose computer, such as a personal computer, can do many different tasks depending on programming.
   a. ADTECH
   b. Embedded system
   c. ACNielsen
   d. AMAX

18. _____ is the set of reasons that determines one to engage in a particular behavior. The term is generally used for human _____ but, theoretically, it can be used to describe the causes for animal behavior as well
   a. Role playing
   b. 180SearchAssistant
   c. Power III
   d. Motivation

19. In algebra, a _____ is a function depending on n that associates a scalar, det(A), to an n×n square matrix A. The fundamental geometric meaning of a _____ is a scale factor for measure when A is regarded as a linear transformation. _____s are important both in calculus, where they enter the substitution rule for several variables, and in multilinear algebra.

For a fixed nonnegative integer n, there is a unique _____ function for the n×n matrices over any commutative ring R. In particular, this function exists when R is the field of real or complex numbers.

   a. Motion Picture Association of America's film-rating system
   b. Black Friday
   c. Package-on-Package
   d. Determinant

20. _____ is a term commonly used to describe commerce transactions between businesses like the one between a manufacturer and a wholesaler or a wholesaler and a retailer i.e both the buyer and the seller are business entity.This is unlike business-to-consumers (B2C) which involve a business entity and end consumer, or business-to-government (B2G) which involve a business entity and government.

Chapter 6. Primary-Data Collection

The volume of B2B transactions is much higher than the volume of B2C transactions. The primary reason for this is that in a typical supply chain there will be many B2B transactions involving subcomponent or raw materials, and only one B2C transaction, specifically sale of the finished product to the end customer.

a. Business-to-business
b. Customer relationship management
c. Disruptive technology
d. Social marketing

21. _____ is the examining of goods or services from retailers with the intent to purchase at that time. _____ is an activity of selection and/or purchase. In some contexts it is considered a leisure activity as well as an economic one.

a. Hawkers
b. Khodebshchik
c. Discount store
d. Shopping

22. _____ is systematic determination of merit, worth, and significance of something or someone using criteria against a set of standards. _____ often is used to characterize and appraise subjects of interest in a wide range of human enterprises, including the arts, criminal justice, foundations and non-profit organizations, government, health care, and other human services.

Depending on the topic of interest, there are professional groups which look to the quality and rigor of the _____ process.

a. ACNielsen
b. ADTECH
c. AMAX
d. Evaluation

23. _____ is a telephone surveying technique in which the interviewer follows a script provided by a software application. The software is able to customize the flow of the questionnaire based on the answers provided, as well as information already known about the participant.

CATI may function in the following manner

- A computerized questionnaire is administered to respondents over the telephone.
- The interviewer sits in front of a computer screen
- Upon command, the computer dials the telephone number to be called.
- When contact is made, the interviewer reads the questions posed on the computer screen and records the respondent's answers directly into the computer.
- Interim and update reports can be compiled instantaneously, as the data are being collected.
- CATI software has built-in logic, which also enhances data accuracy.
- The program will personalize questions and control for logically incorrect answers, such as percentage answers that do not add up to 100 percent.
- The software has built-in branching logic, which will skip questions that are not applicable or will probe for more detail when warranted.

a. Computer-assisted telephone interviewing
b. 6-3-5 Brainwriting
c. Power III
d. 180SearchAssistant

24. In economics, business, retail, and accounting, a _____ is the value of money that has been used up to produce something, and hence is not available for use anymore. In economics, a _____ is an alternative that is given up as a result of a decision. In business, the _____ may be one of acquisition, in which case the amount of money expended to acquire it is counted as _____.
   a. Variable cost
   b. Fixed costs
   c. Cost
   d. Transaction cost

25. _____, known also as _____ entification (Caller IDD) is a telephone service, available on POTS (Plain Old Telephone Service) lines, that transmits a caller's number to the called party's telephone equipment during the ringing signal _____ can also provide a name associated with the calling telephone number, for a higher fee. The information made available to the called party may be made visible on a telephone's own display or on a separate attached device.
   a. Power III
   b. Caller ID
   c. 6-3-5 Brainwriting
   d. 180SearchAssistant

26. _____ is a sampling technique used when 'natural' groupings are evident in a statistical population. It is often used in marketing research. In this technique, the total population is divided into these groups (or clusters) and a sample of the groups is selected.
   a. Power III
   b. Snowball sampling
   c. Cluster sampling
   d. Quota sampling

27. _____ is a type of nonprobability sampling which involves the sample being drawn from that part of the population which is close to hand. That is, a sample population selected because it is readily available and convenient. The researcher using such a sample cannot scientifically make generalizations about the total population from this sample because it would not be representative enough.
   a. ACNielsen
   b. ADTECH
   c. Accidental sampling
   d. AMAX

28. Sampling is the use of a subset of the population to represent the whole population. Probability sampling, or random sampling, is a sampling technique in which the probability of getting any particular sample may be calculated. _____ does not meet this criterion and should be used with caution.
   a. Quota sampling
   b. Snowball sampling
   c. Power III
   d. Nonprobability sampling

29. In _____, the population is first segmented into mutually exclusive sub-groups, just as in stratified sampling. Then judgment is used to select the subjects or units from each segment based on a specified proportion. For example, an interviewer may be told to sample 200 females and 300 males between the age of 45 and 60.
   a. Snowball sampling
   b. Quota sampling
   c. Power III
   d. Nonprobability sampling

Chapter 6. Primary-Data Collection

30. In statistics, a simple random sample is a subset of individuals (a sample) chosen from a larger set (a population.) Each individual is chosen randomly and entirely by chance, such that each individual has the same probability of being chosen at any stage during the sampling process, and each subset of k individuals has the same probability of being chosen for the sample as any other subset of k individuals (.) This process and technique is known as _____, and should not be confused with Random Sampling.
    a. Logit analysis
    b. Market analysis
    c. Focus group
    d. Simple random sampling

31. _____ is a statistical method involving the selection of elements from an ordered sampling frame. The most common form of _____ is an equal-probability method, in which every kth element in the frame is selected, where k, the sampling interval (sometimes known as the 'skip'), is calculated as:

    sample size (n) = population size (N) /k

Using this procedure each element in the population has a known and equal probability of selection. This makes _____ functionally similar to simple random sampling.

    a. Selection bias
    b. Power III
    c. 180SearchAssistant
    d. Systematic sampling

32. In finance, an _____ is a contract between a buyer and a seller that gives the buyer the right--but not the obligation--to buy or to sell a particular asset (the underlying asset) at a later day at an agreed price. In return for granting the _____, the seller collects a payment (the premium) from the buyer. A call _____ gives the buyer the right to buy the underlying asset; a put _____ gives the buyer of the _____ the right to sell the underlying asset.
    a. Option
    b. AMAX
    c. ACNielsen
    d. ADTECH

33. _____ is that part of statistical practice concerned with the selection of individual observations intended to yield some knowledge about a population of concern, especially for the purposes of statistical inference. Each observation measures one or more properties (weight, location, etc.) of an observable entity enumerated to distinguish objects or individuals.
    a. AStore
    b. Sports Marketing Group
    c. Richard Buckminster 'Bucky' Fuller
    d. Sampling

34. _____ is a standard point of view or personal prejudice. especially when the tendency interferes with the ability to be impartial, unprejudiced, or objective. The term _____ed is used to describe an action, judgment, or other outcome influenced by a prejudged perspective.
    a. 180SearchAssistant
    b. Bias
    c. Power III
    d. 6-3-5 Brainwriting

Chapter 6. Primary-Data Collection

35. _____ is difficult to define. For example, in 1952, Alfred Kroeber and Clyde Kluckhohn compiled a list of 164 definitions of '_____' in _____: A Critical Review of Concepts and Definitions. However, the word '_____' is most commonly used in three basic senses:

- excellence of taste in the fine arts and humanities
- an integrated pattern of human knowledge, belief, and behavior that depends upon the capacity for symbolic thought and social learning
- the set of shared attitudes, values, goals, and practices that characterizes an institution, organization or group.

When the concept first emerged in eighteenth- and nineteenth-century Europe, it connoted a process of cultivation or improvement, as in agriculture or horticulture. In the nineteenth century, it came to refer first to the betterment or refinement of the individual, especially through education, and then to the fulfillment of national aspirations or ideals.

a. Culture
c. African Americans
b. AStore
d. Albert Einstein

36. _____ describes the situation when output from (or information about the result of) an event or phenomenon in the past will influence the same event/phenomenon in the present or future. When an event is part of a chain of cause-and-effect that forms a circuit or loop, then the event is said to 'feed back' into itself.

_____ is also a synonym for:

- _____ Signal; the information about the initial event that is the basis for subsequent modification of the event.
- _____ Loop; the causal path that leads from the initial generation of the _____ signal to the subsequent modification of the event.

_____ is a mechanism, process or signal that is looped back to control a system within itself. Such a loop is called a _____ loop.

a. Feedback
c. 180SearchAssistant
b. Power III
d. 6-3-5 Brainwriting

37. _____ is a contract between two parties, one being the employer and the other being the employee. An employee may be defined as: 'A person in the service of another under any contract of hire, express or implied, oral or written, where the employer has the power or right to control and direct the employee in the material details of how the work is to be performed.' Black's Law Dictionary page 471 (5th ed. 1979.)

a. Employment
c. AMAX
b. ADTECH
d. ACNielsen

38. _____ or Mystery Consumer is a tool used by market research companies to measure quality of retail service or gather specific information about products and services. Mystery shoppers posing as normal customers perform specific tasks-- such as purchasing a product, asking questions, registering complaints or behaving in a certain way - and then provide detailed reports or feedback about their experiences.

_____ began in the 1940s as a way to measure employee integrity.

   a. Market research
   c. Mystery shopping
   b. Questionnaire
   d. Mystery shoppers

39. In economics and sociology, an _____ is any factor (financial or non-financial) that enables or motivates a particular course of action, or counts as a reason for preferring one choice to the alternatives. It is an expectation that encourages people to behave in a certain way. Since human beings are purposeful creatures, the study of _____ structures is central to the study of all economic activity (both in terms of individual decision-making and in terms of co-operation and competition within a larger institutional structure.)
   a. ACNielsen
   c. AMAX
   b. Incentive
   d. ADTECH

40. A _____ is a tool used to measure the viewing habits of TV and cable audiences.

The _____ is a 'box', about the size of a paperback book. The box is hooked up to each television set and is accompanied by a remote control unit.

   a. Power III
   c. People meter
   b. 6-3-5 Brainwriting
   d. 180SearchAssistant

41. A '_____' or television commercial (often just commercial (US) or advert or ad (UK) or ad-film (India)) is a span of television programming produced and paid for by an organisation that conveys a message. Advertisement revenue provides a significant portion of the funding for most privately owned television networks. The vast majority of _____s today consist of brief advertising spots, ranging in length from a few seconds to several minutes (as well as program-length infomercials.)
   a. Ghost sign
   c. Radio commercial
   b. Transit media
   d. Television advertisement

42. _____ in economics and business is the result of an exchange and from that trade we assign a numerical monetary value to a good, service or asset. If I trade 4 apples for an orange, the _____ of an orange is 4 - apples. Inversely, the _____ of an apple is 1/4 oranges.
   a. Discounts and allowances
   c. Contribution margin-based pricing
   b. Price
   d. Pricing

43. _____ is the ability of an individual or group to seclude themselves or information about themselves and thereby reveal themselves selectively. The boundaries and content of what is considered private differ among cultures and individuals, but share basic common themes. _____ is sometimes related to anonymity, the wish to remain unnoticed or unidentified in the public realm.
   a. Power III
   c. 180SearchAssistant
   b. 6-3-5 Brainwriting
   d. Privacy

Chapter 6. Primary-Data Collection

44. _____ is a business discipline which is focused on the practical application of marketing techniques and the management of a firm's marketing resources and activities. Marketing managers are often responsible for influencing the level, timing, and composition of customer demand accepted definition of the term. In part, this is because the role of a marketing manager can vary significantly based on a business' size, corporate culture, and industry context.

   a. Business structure   b. Marketing management
   c. Performance-based advertising   d. Door-to-door

45. _____ is a broad label that refers to any individuals or households that use goods and services generated within the economy. The concept of a _____ is used in different contexts, so that the usage and significance of the term may vary.

A _____ is a person who uses any product or service.

   a. 180SearchAssistant   b. 6-3-5 Brainwriting
   c. Power III   d. Consumer

46. _____ is one of the four elements of marketing mix. An organization or set of organizations (go-betweens) involved in the process of making a product or service available for use or consumption by a consumer or business user.

The other three parts of the marketing mix are product, pricing, and promotion.

   a. Better Living Through Chemistry   b. Japan Advertising Photographers' Association
   c. Distribution   d. Comparison-Shopping agent

Chapter 7. Qualitative Research

1. An _____ is one type of focus group, and is a sub-set of online research methods.

A moderator invites prescreened, qualified respondents who represent the target of interest to log on to conferencing software at a pre-arranged time and to take part in an _____. Some researchers will offer incentives for participating but this raises a number of ethical questions.

 a. Automated surveys
 b. Intangibility
 c. Engagement
 d. Online focus group

2. A _____ is a form of qualitative research in which a group of people are asked about their attitude towards a product, service, concept, advertisement, idea, or packaging. Questions are asked in an interactive group setting where participants are free to talk with other group members.

Ernest Dichter originated the idea of having a 'group therapy' for products and this process is what became known as a _____.

 a. Cross tabulation
 b. Logit analysis
 c. Focus group
 d. Marketing research process

3. _____ is defined by the American _____ Association as the activity, set of institutions, and processes for creating, communicating, delivering, and exchanging offerings that have value for customers, clients, partners, and society at large. The term developed from the original meaning which referred literally to going to market, as in shopping, or going to a market to sell goods or services.

_____ practice tends to be seen as a creative industry, which includes advertising, distribution and selling.

 a. Marketing
 b. Marketing myopia
 c. Customer acquisition management
 d. Product naming

4. Consumer market research is a form of applied sociology that concentrates on understanding the behaviours, whims and preferences, of consumers in a market-based economy, and aims to understand the effects and comparative success of marketing campaigns. The field of consumer _____ as a statistical science was pioneered by Arthur Nielsen with the founding of the ACNielsen Company in 1923 .

Thus _____ is the systematic and objective identification, collection, analysis, and dissemination of information for the purpose of assisting management in decision making related to the identification and solution of problems and opportunities in marketing.

 a. Marketing research process
 b. Focus group
 c. Logit analysis
 d. Marketing research

5. _____ is a set of six steps which defines the tasks to be accomplished in conducting a marketing research study. These include problem definition, developing an approach to problem, research design formulation, field work, data preparation and analysis, and report generation and presentation.
 a. Preference-rank translation
 b. Market analysis
 c. Marketing research process
 d. Simple random sampling

Chapter 7. Qualitative Research

6. _____ is a field of inquiry that crosscuts disciplines and subject matters. _____ers aim to gather an in-depth understanding of human behavior and the reasons that govern such behavior. The discipline investigates the why and how of decision making, not just what, where, when.
   a. 6-3-5 Brainwriting
   b. Power III
   c. 180SearchAssistant
   d. Qualitative research

7. A _____ attribute is one that exists in a range of magnitudes, and can therefore be measured. Measurements of any particular _____ property are expressed as a specific quantity, referred to as a unit, multiplied by a number. Examples of physical quantities are distance, mass, and time.
   a. Lifestyle city
   b. Dolly Dimples
   c. BeyondROI
   d. Quantitative

8. A _____ is a research instrument consisting of a series of questions and other prompts for the purpose of gathering information from respondents. Although they are often designed for statistical analysis of the responses, this is not always the case. The _____ was invented by Sir Francis Galton.
   a. Mystery shoppers
   b. Market research
   c. Mystery shopping
   d. Questionnaire

9. _____ or _____ data refers to selected population characteristics as used in government, marketing or opinion research, or the _____ profiles used in such research. Note the distinction from the term 'demography' Commonly-used _____ include race, age, income, disabilities, mobility (in terms of travel time to work or number of vehicles available), educational attainment, home ownership, employment status, and even location.
   a. African Americans
   b. AStore
   c. Albert Einstein
   d. Demographic

10. _____s are used in open sentences. For instance, in the formula $x + 1 = 5$, x is a _____ which represents an 'unknown' number. _____s are often represented by letters of the Roman alphabet, or those of other alphabets, such as Greek, and use other special symbols.
    a. Book of business
    b. Quantitative
    c. Personalization
    d. Variable

11. _____ is either an activity of a living being (such as a human), consisting of receiving knowledge of the outside world through the senses, or the recording of data using scientific instruments. The term may also refer to any datum collected during this activity.

The scientific method requires _____s of nature to formulate and test hypotheses.

   a. AMAX
   b. ACNielsen
   c. ADTECH
   d. Observation

12. _____ is the conveying of events in words, images, and sounds often by improvisation or embellishment. Stories or narratives have been shared in every culture and in every land as a means of entertainment, education, preservation of culture and in order to instill moral values. Crucial elements of stories and _____ include plot and characters, as well as the narrative point of view.

a. 180SearchAssistant
c. Storytelling
b. 6-3-5 Brainwriting
d. Power III

13. In economics, business, retail, and accounting, a _____ is the value of money that has been used up to produce something, and hence is not available for use anymore. In economics, a _____ is an alternative that is given up as a result of a decision. In business, the _____ may be one of acquisition, in which case the amount of money expended to acquire it is counted as _____.
   a. Cost
   c. Variable cost
   b. Transaction cost
   d. Fixed costs

14. _____ refer to a collection of facts usually collected as the result of experience, observation or experiment or a set of premises. This may consist of numbers, words particularly as measurements or observations of a set of variables. _____ are often viewed as a lowest level of abstraction from which information and knowledge are derived.
   a. Sample size
   c. Mean
   b. Pearson product-moment correlation coefficient
   d. Data

15. _____ is a broad label that refers to any individuals or households that use goods and services generated within the economy. The concept of a _____ is used in different contexts, so that the usage and significance of the term may vary.

A _____ is a person who uses any product or service.

   a. Consumer
   c. 180SearchAssistant
   b. 6-3-5 Brainwriting
   d. Power III

16. _____ in organizations and public policy is both the organizational process of creating and maintaining a plan; and the psychological process of thinking about the activities required to create a desired goal on some scale. As such, it is a fundamental property of intelligent behavior. This thought process is essential to the creation and refinement of a plan, or integration of it with other plans, that is, it combines forecasting of developments with the preparation of scenarios of how to react to them.
   a. 180SearchAssistant
   c. Planning
   b. Power III
   d. 6-3-5 Brainwriting

17. Advertising mail junk mail is the delivery of advertising material to recipients of postal mail. The delivery of advertising mail forms a large and growing service for many postal services, and _____ marketing forms a significant portion of the direct marketing industry. Some organizations attempt to help people opt-out of receiving advertising mail, in many cases motivated by a concern over its negative environmental impact.
   a. Directory Harvest Attack
   c. Telemarketing
   b. Phishing
   d. Direct mail

18. _____ refers to the methods, practices and operations conducted to promote and sustain certain categories of commercial activity. The term is understood to have different specific meanings depending on the context. Merchandise is a sale goods at a store

In marketing, one of the definitions of _____ is the practice in which the brand or image from one product or service is used to sell another.

Chapter 7. Qualitative Research

a. New Media Strategies
b. Word of mouth
c. Marketing communication
d. Merchandising

19. _____ is the process of finding associated geographic coordinates (often expressed as latitude and longitude) from other geographic data, such as street addresses or the coordinates can be embedded into media such as digital photographs via geotagging.

Reverse _____ is the opposite: finding an associated textual location such as a street address, from geographic coordinates.

a. 6-3-5 Brainwriting
b. 180SearchAssistant
c. Power III
d. Geocoding

20. _____ are used to collect quantitative information about items in a population. Surveys of human populations and institutions are common in political polling and government, health, social science and marketing research. A survey may focus on opinions or factual information depending on its purpose, and many surveys involve administering questions to individuals.

a. Convergent
b. Statistical surveys
c. BeyondROI
d. Gross Margin Return on Inventory Investment

21. A personal and cultural _____ is a relative ethic _____, an assumption upon which implementation can be extrapolated. A _____ system is a set of consistent _____s and measures that is soo not true. A principle _____ is a foundation upon which other _____s and measures of integrity are based.

a. Package-on-Package
b. Perceptual maps
c. Supreme Court of the United States
d. Value

22. _____ describes the situation when output from (or information about the result of) an event or phenomenon in the past will influence the same event/phenomenon in the present or future. When an event is part of a chain of cause-and-effect that forms a circuit or loop, then the event is said to 'feed back' into itself.

_____ is also a synonym for:

- _____ Signal; the information about the initial event that is the basis for subsequent modification of the event.
- _____ Loop; the causal path that leads from the initial generation of the _____ signal to the subsequent modification of the event.

_____ is a mechanism, process or signal that is looped back to control a system within itself. Such a loop is called a _____ loop.

a. 6-3-5 Brainwriting
b. Power III
c. 180SearchAssistant
d. Feedback

23. _____ is a term used to describe a process of preparing and collecting data - for example as part of a process improvement or similar project.

Chapter 7. Qualitative Research 55

_____ usually takes place early on in an improvement project, and is often formalised through a _____ Plan which often contains the following activity.

1. Pre collection activity - Agree goals, target data, definitions, methods
2. Collection - _____
3. Present Findings - usually involves some form of sorting analysis and/or presentation.

A formal _____ process is necessary as it ensures that data gathered is both defined and accurate and that subsequent decisions based on arguments embodied in the findings are valid . The process provides both a baseline from which to measure from and in certain cases a target on what to improve. Types of _____ 1-By mail questionnaires 2-By personal interview

- Six sigma
- Sampling (statistics)

a. 180SearchAssistant
b. Data collection
c. 6-3-5 Brainwriting
d. Power III

24. _____ is a common word game involving an exchange of words that are associated together.

Once an original word has been chosen, usually randomly or arbitrarily, a player will find a word that they associate with it and make it known to all the players, usually by saying it aloud or writing it down as the next item on a list of words so far used. The next player must then do the same with this previous word.

a. Power III
b. Word association
c. 6-3-5 Brainwriting
d. 180SearchAssistant

25. _____ is a group creativity technique designed to generate a large number of ideas for the solution of a problem. The method was first popularized in the late 1930s by Alex Faickney Osborn in a book called Applied Imagination. Osborn proposed that groups could double their creative output with _____.
a. Albert Einstein
b. Brainstorming
c. AStore
d. African Americans

26. In economics, an externality or spillover of an economic transaction is an impact on a party that is not directly involved in the transaction. In such a case, prices do not reflect the full costs or benefits in production or consumption of a product or service. A positive impact is called an _____ benefit, while a negative impact is called an _____ cost.
a. ACNielsen
b. ADTECH
c. External
d. AMAX

27. The Oxford University Press defines _____ as 'marketing on a worldwide scale reconciling or taking commercial advantage of global operational differences, similarities and opportunities in order to meet global objectives.' Oxford University Press' Glossary of Marketing Terms.

Chapter 7. Qualitative Research

Here are three reasons for the shift from domestic to _____ as given by the authors of the textbook, _____ Management--3rd Edition by Masaaki Kotabe and Kristiaan Helsen, 2004.

One of the product categories in which global competition has been easy to track is in U.S. automotive sales.

a. Diversity marketing
c. Digital marketing
b. Guerrilla Marketing
d. Global marketing

28. _____ refers to the production of some commodity or service, such as a television program, using a company's own funds, staff, or resources.

This is in contrast to production being outsourced (contracted out) to another company.

- Proprietary

a. Outsourcing
c. ACNielsen
b. Intangible assets
d. In-house

29. _____ are a class of semi-structured projective techniques. _____ typically provide respondents with beginnings of sentences, referred to as 'stems,' and respondents then complete the sentences in ways that are meaningful to them. The responses are believed to provide indications of attitudes, beliefs, motivations, or other mental states.
a. Sentence completion tests
c. Response rate
b. Reference value
d. Power III

30. The _____ is an example of a projective test.

Historically, the _____ or _____ has been amongst the most widely used, researched, and taught projective psychological tests. Its adherents claim that it taps a subject's unconscious to reveal repressed aspects of personality, motives and needs for achievement, power and intimacy, and problem-solving abilities.

a. 6-3-5 Brainwriting
c. Power III
b. 180SearchAssistant
d. Thematic apperception test

31. A _____ is a subgroup of people or organizations sharing one or more characteristics that cause them to have similar product and/or service needs. A true _____ meets all of the following criteria: it is distinct from other segments (different segments have different needs), it is homogeneous within the segment (exhibits common needs); it responds similarly to a market stimulus, and it can be reached by a market intervention. The term is also used when consumers with identical product and/or service needs are divided up into groups so they can be charged different amounts.
a. Commercial planning
c. Production orientation
b. Market segment
d. Customer insight

32. _____ is a business term meaning the market segment to which a particular good or service is marketed. It is mainly defined by age, gender, geography, socio-economic grouping, technographic, or any other combination of demographics. It is generally studied and mapped by an organization through lists and reports containing demographic information that may have an effect on the marketing of key products or services.
   a. Brando
   b. Category Development Index
   c. Distribution
   d. Market specialization

Chapter 8. Experimentation in Marketing Research

1. _____ describes data and characteristics about the population or phenomenon being studied. _____ answers the questions who, what, where, when and how.

Although the data description is factual, accurate and systematic, the research cannot describe what caused a situation.

   a. Power III
   b. Two-tailed test
   c. Sampling error
   d. Descriptive research

2. _____ in economics and business is the result of an exchange and from that trade we assign a numerical monetary value to a good, service or asset. If I trade 4 apples for an orange, the _____ of an orange is 4 - apples. Inversely, the _____ of an apple is 1/4 oranges.
   a. Discounts and allowances
   b. Pricing
   c. Contribution margin-based pricing
   d. Price

3. _____s are used in open sentences. For instance, in the formula x + 1 = 5, x is a _____ which represents an 'unknown' number. _____s are often represented by letters of the Roman alphabet, or those of other alphabets, such as Greek, and use other special symbols.
   a. Book of business
   b. Personalization
   c. Variable
   d. Quantitative

4. _____ is a telephone surveying technique in which the interviewer follows a script provided by a software application. The software is able to customize the flow of the questionnaire based on the answers provided, as well as information already known about the participant.

CATI may function in the following manner

- A computerized questionnaire is administered to respondents over the telephone.
- The interviewer sits in front of a computer screen
- Upon command, the computer dials the telephone number to be called.
- When contact is made, the interviewer reads the questions posed on the computer screen and records the respondent's answers directly into the computer.
- Interim and update reports can be compiled instantaneously, as the data are being collected.
- CATI software has built-in logic, which also enhances data accuracy.
- The program will personalize questions and control for logically incorrect answers, such as percentage answers that do not add up to 100 percent.
- The software has built-in branching logic, which will skip questions that are not applicable or will probe for more detail when warranted.

   a. 6-3-5 Brainwriting
   b. 180SearchAssistant
   c. Power III
   d. Computer-assisted telephone interviewing

5. _____ denotes a necessary relationship between one event and another event (called effect) which is the direct consequence of the first.

Chapter 8. Experimentation in Marketing Research

While this informal understanding suffices in everyday use, the philosophical analysis of how best to characterize _____ extends over millennia. In the western philosophical tradition explicit discussion stretches back at least as far as Aristotle, and the topic remains a staple in contemporary philosophy journals.

a. Power III
c. 6-3-5 Brainwriting
b. 180SearchAssistant
d. Causality

6. _____ is defined by the American _____ Association as the activity, set of institutions, and processes for creating, communicating, delivering, and exchanging offerings that have value for customers, clients, partners, and society at large. The term developed from the original meaning which referred literally to going to market, as in shopping, or going to a market to sell goods or services.

_____ practice tends to be seen as a creative industry, which includes advertising, distribution and selling.

a. Marketing
c. Customer acquisition management
b. Product naming
d. Marketing myopia

7. A _____ applies the scientific method to experimentally examine an intervention in the real world (or as many experimental economists like to say, naturally-occurring environments) rather than in the laboratory. _____s, like lab experiments, generally randomize subjects (or other sampling units) into treatment and control groups and compare outcomes between these groups. Clinical trials of pharmaceuticals are one example of _____s.

a. Response variable
c. 180SearchAssistant
b. Power III
d. Field experiment

8. In economics, an externality or spillover of an economic transaction is an impact on a party that is not directly involved in the transaction. In such a case, prices do not reflect the full costs or benefits in production or consumption of a product or service. A positive impact is called an _____ benefit, while a negative impact is called an _____ cost.

a. ADTECH
c. AMAX
b. External
d. ACNielsen

9. _____ is the validity of generalized (causal) inferences in scientific studies, usually based on experiments as experimental validity.

Inferences about cause-effect relationships based on a specific scientific study are said to possess _____ if they may be generalized from the unique and idiosyncratic settings, procedures and participants to other populations and conditions Causal inferences said to possess high degrees of _____ can reasonably be expected to apply (a) to the target population of the study (i.e. from which the sample was drawn) (also referred to as population validity), and (b) to the universe of other populations (e.g. across time and space.)

The most common loss of _____ comes from the fact that experiments using human participants often employ small samples obtained from a single geographic location or with idiosyncratic features (e.g. volunteers.)

a. ACNielsen
c. AMAX
b. ADTECH
d. External validity

Chapter 8. Experimentation in Marketing Research

10. _____ is the validity of (causal) inferences in scientific studies, usually based on experiments as experimental validity .

Inferences are said to possess _____ if a causal relation between two variables is properly demonstrated . A causal inference may be based on a relation when three criteria are satisfied:

1. the 'cause' precedes the 'effect' in time (temporal precedence),
2. the 'cause' and the 'effect' are related (covariation), and
3. there are no plausible alternative explanations for the observed covariation (nonspuriousness) .

In scientific experimental settings, researchers often manipulate a variable (the independent variable) to see what effect it has on a second variable (the dependent variable) For example, a researcher might, for different experimental groups, manipulate the dosage of a particular drug between groups to see what effect it has on health. In this example, the researcher wants to make a causal inference, namely, that different doses of the drug may be held responsible for observed changes or differences.

a. ADTECH
b. AMAX
c. ACNielsen
d. Internal validity

11. In economics, business, retail, and accounting, a _____ is the value of money that has been used up to produce something, and hence is not available for use anymore. In economics, a _____ is an alternative that is given up as a result of a decision. In business, the _____ may be one of acquisition, in which case the amount of money expended to acquire it is counted as _____.

a. Variable cost
b. Cost
c. Fixed costs
d. Transaction cost

12. Competitiveness is a comparative concept of the ability and performance of a firm, sub-sector or country to sell and supply goods and/or services in a given market. Although widely used in economics and business management, the usefulness of the concept, particularly in the context of national competitiveness, is vigorously disputed by economists, such as Paul Krugman .

The term may also be applied to markets, where it is used to refer to the extent to which the market structure may be regarded as perfectly _____.

a. Geographical pricing
b. Customs union
c. Free trade zone
d. Competitive

13. A _____, in the field of business and marketing, is a geographic region or demographic group used to gauge the viability of a product or service in the mass market prior to a wide scale roll-out. The criteria used to judge the acceptability of a _____ region or group include:

1. a population that is demographically similar to the proposed target market; and
2. relative isolation from densely populated media markets so that advertising to the test audience can be efficient and economical.

Chapter 8. Experimentation in Marketing Research 61

The _____ ideally aims to duplicate 'everything' - promotion and distribution as well as `product' - on a smaller scale. The technique replicates, typically in one area, what is planned to occur in a national launch; and the results are very carefully monitored, so that they can be extrapolated to projected national results. The `area' may be any one of the following:

- Television area
- Test town
- Residential neighborhood
- Test site

A number of decisions have to be taken about any _____:

- Which _____?
- What is to be tested?
- How long a test?
- What are the success criteria?

The simple go or no-go decision, together with the related reduction of risk, is normally the main justification for the expense of _____s. At the same time, however, such _____s can be used to test specific elements of a new product's marketing mix; possibly the version of the product itself, the promotional message and media spend, the distribution channels and the price.

a. 180SearchAssistant
b. Power III
c. Preadolescence
d. Test market

14. _____ is a concept that denotes the precise probability of specific eventualities. Technically, the notion of _____ is independent from the notion of value and, as such, eventualities may have both beneficial and adverse consequences. However, in general usage the convention is to focus only on potential negative impact to some characteristic of value that may arise from a future event.
a. Risk
b. Power III
c. 6-3-5 Brainwriting
d. 180SearchAssistant

15. _____ is the imitation of some real thing, state of affairs, or process. The act of simulating something generally entails representing certain key characteristics or behaviors of a selected physical or abstract system.

_____ is used in many contexts, including the modeling of natural systems or human systems in order to gain insight into their functioning.

a. 180SearchAssistant
b. 6-3-5 Brainwriting
c. Power III
d. Simulation

16. _____ refer to a collection of facts usually collected as the result of experience, observation or experiment or a set of premises. This may consist of numbers, words particularly as measurements or observations of a set of variables. _____ are often viewed as a lowest level of abstraction from which information and knowledge are derived.

a. Sample size
b. Pearson product-moment correlation coefficient
c. Mean
d. Data

17. _____ is the process of finding associated geographic coordinates (often expressed as latitude and longitude) from other geographic data, such as street addresses or the coordinates can be embedded into media such as digital photographs via geotagging.

Reverse _____ is the opposite: finding an associated textual location such as a street address, from geographic coordinates.

a. 6-3-5 Brainwriting
b. Power III
c. Geocoding
d. 180SearchAssistant

18. _____ is one of the four Ps of the marketing mix. The other three aspects are product, promotion, and place. It is also a key variable in microeconomic price allocation theory.

a. Relationship based pricing
b. Pricing
c. Price
d. Competitor indexing

19. _____ is a process of gathering, modeling, and transforming data with the goal of highlighting useful information, suggesting conclusions, and supporting decision making. _____ has multiple facets and approaches, encompassing diverse techniques under a variety of names, in different business, science, and social science domains.

Data mining is a particular _____ technique that focuses on modeling and knowledge discovery for predictive rather than purely descriptive purposes.

a. Power III
b. 6-3-5 Brainwriting
c. 180SearchAssistant
d. Data analysis

20. Advertising mail junk mail is the delivery of advertising material to recipients of postal mail. The delivery of advertising mail forms a large and growing service for many postal services, and _____ marketing forms a significant portion of the direct marketing industry. Some organizations attempt to help people opt-out of receiving advertising mail, in many cases motivated by a concern over its negative environmental impact.

a. Direct mail
b. Phishing
c. Telemarketing
d. Directory Harvest Attack

21. A _____ is a research instrument consisting of a series of questions and other prompts for the purpose of gathering information from respondents. Although they are often designed for statistical analysis of the responses, this is not always the case. The _____ was invented by Sir Francis Galton.

a. Market research
b. Mystery shopping
c. Mystery shoppers
d. Questionnaire

22. _____ or _____ data refers to selected population characteristics as used in government, marketing or opinion research, or the _____ profiles used in such research. Note the distinction from the term 'demography' Commonly-used _____ include race, age, income, disabilities, mobility (in terms of travel time to work or number of vehicles available), educational attainment, home ownership, employment status, and even location.

| a. AStore | b. Albert Einstein |
| c. African Americans | d. Demographic |

23. _____ is the study of the Earth and its lands, features, inhabitants, and phenomena. A literal translation would be 'to describe or write about the Earth'. The first person to use the word '_____' was Eratosthenes.

| a. Power III | b. 6-3-5 Brainwriting |
| c. Geography | d. 180SearchAssistant |

24. _____ is that part of statistical practice concerned with the selection of individual observations intended to yield some knowledge about a population of concern, especially for the purposes of statistical inference. Each observation measures one or more properties (weight, location, etc.) of an observable entity enumerated to distinguish objects or individuals.

| a. Richard Buckminster 'Bucky' Fuller | b. AStore |
| c. Sports Marketing Group | d. Sampling |

25. _____ is a standard point of view or personal prejudice. especially when the tendency interferes with the ability to be impartial, unprejudiced, or objective. The term _____ed is used to describe an action, judgment, or other outcome influenced by a prejudged perspective.

| a. Bias | b. Power III |
| c. 6-3-5 Brainwriting | d. 180SearchAssistant |

26. In statistics, an _____ is a term in a statistical model added when the effect of two or more variables is not simply additive. Such a term reflects that the effect of one variable depends on the values of one or more other variables.

Thus, for a response Y and two variables x_1 and x_2 an additive model would be:

$$Y = ax_1 + bx_2 + \text{error}$$

In contrast to this,

$$Y = ax_1 + bx_2 + c(x_1 \times x_2) + \text{error},$$

is an example of a model with an _____ between variables x_1 and x_2 ('error' refers to the random variable whose value by which y differs from the expected value of y.)

| a. ADTECH | b. AMAX |
| c. ACNielsen | d. Interaction |

27. In social science and psychometrics, _____ refers to whether a scale measures or correlates with a theorized psychological construct (such as 'fluid intelligence'.) It is related to the theoretical ideas behind the personality trait under consideration; a non-existent concept in the physical sense may be suggested as a method of organising how personality can be viewed. The unobservable idea of a unidimensional easier-to-harder dimension must be 'constructed' in the words of human language and graphics.

Chapter 8. Experimentation in Marketing Research

a. Criterion validity
c. Discriminant validity
b. Predictive validity
d. Construct validity

28. In psychometrics, _____ refers to the extent to which a measure represents all facets of a given social construct. For example, a depression scale may lack _____ if it only assesses the affective dimension of depression but fails to take into account the behavioral dimension. An element of subjectivity exists in relation to determining _____, which requires a degree of agreement about what a particular personality trait such as extraversion represents.

a. Criterion validity
c. Predictive validity
b. Convergent validity
d. Content validity

29. In the absence of a more specific context, convergence denotes the approach toward a definite value, as time goes on; or to a definite point, a common view or opinion, or toward a fixed or equilibrium state. _____ is the adjectival form, and also a noun meaning an iterative approximation.

In mathematics, convergence describes limiting behaviour, particularly of an infinite sequence or series, toward some limit.

a. Geo
c. Convergent
b. Good things come to those who wait
d. Strict liability

30. _____ is the degree to which an operation is similar to (converges on) other operations that it theoretically should also be similar to. For instance, to show the _____ of a test of mathematics skills, the scores on the test can be correlated with scores on other tests that are also designed to measure basic mathematics ability. High correlations between the test scores would be evidence of a _____.

a. Discriminant validity
c. Content validity
b. Criterion validity
d. Convergent validity

31. In algebra, the _____ of a polynomial with real or complex coefficients is a certain expression in the coefficients of the polynomial which is equal to zero if and only if the polynomial has a multiple root (i.e. a root with multiplicity greater than one) in the complex numbers. For example, the _____ of the quadratic polynomial

$$ax^2 + bx + c \text{ is } b^2 - 4ac.$$

The _____ of the cubic polynomial

$$ax^3 + bx^2 + cx + d \text{ is } b^2c^2 - 4ac^3 - 4b^3d - 27a^2d^2 + 18abcd.$$

a. Flighting
c. Lifestyle center
b. Consumption Map
d. Discriminant

32. _____ describes the degree to which the operationalization is not similar to (diverges from) other operationalizations that it theoretically should not be similar to.

Campbell and Fiske (1959) introduced the concept of _____ within their discussion on evaluating test validity. They stressed the importance of using both discriminant and convergent validation techniques when assessing new tests.

 a. Predictive validity
 b. Discriminant validity
 c. Criterion validity
 d. Convergent validity

33. _____ are used to collect quantitative information about items in a population. Surveys of human populations and institutions are common in political polling and government, health, social science and marketing research. A survey may focus on opinions or factual information depending on its purpose, and many surveys involve administering questions to individuals.
 a. Convergent
 b. Gross Margin Return on Inventory Investment
 c. BeyondROI
 d. Statistical surveys

34. A _____ is a statement or claim that a particular event will occur in the future in more certain terms than a forecast. The etymology of this word is Latin . In regards to predicting the future Howard H. Stevenson Says, ' _____ is at least two things: Important and hard.' Important, because we have to act, and hard because we have to realize the future we want, and what is the best way to get there.
 a. Power III
 b. 6-3-5 Brainwriting
 c. 180SearchAssistant
 d. Prediction

35. In psychometrics, _____ is the extent to which a score on a scale or test predicts scores on some criterion measure.

For example, the validity of a cognitive test for job performance is the correlation between test scores and, for example, supervisor performance ratings. Such a cognitive test would have _____ if the observed correlation were statistically significant.

 a. Convergent validity
 b. Predictive validity
 c. Criterion validity
 d. Discriminant validity

36. _____ is a form of communication that typically attempts to persuade potential customers to purchase or to consume more of a particular brand of product or service. 'While now central to the contemporary global economy and the reproduction of global production networks, it is only quite recently that _____ has been more than a marginal influence on patterns of sales and production. The formation of modern _____ was intimately bound up with the emergence of new forms of monopoly capitalism around the end of the 19th and beginning of the 20th century as one element in corporate strategies to create, organize and where possible control markets, especially for mass produced consumer goods.
 a. AMAX
 b. ADTECH
 c. Advertising
 d. ACNielsen

37. Consumer market research is a form of applied sociology that concentrates on understanding the behaviours, whims and preferences, of consumers in a market-based economy, and aims to understand the effects and comparative success of marketing campaigns. The field of consumer _____ as a statistical science was pioneered by Arthur Nielsen with the founding of the ACNielsen Company in 1923 .

Thus _____ is the systematic and objective identification, collection, analysis, and dissemination of information for the purpose of assisting management in decision making related to the identification and solution of problems and opportunities in marketing.

- a. Focus group
- b. Logit analysis
- c. Marketing research process
- d. Marketing research

38. The terms '_____' and 'independent variable' are used in similar but subtly different ways in mathematics and statistics as part of the standard terminology in those subjects. They are used to distinguish between two types of quantities being considered, separating them into those available at the start of a process and those being created by it, where the latter (_____s) are dependent on the former (independent variables.)

In traditional calculus, a function is defined as a relation between two terms called variables because their values vary.

- a. Power III
- b. Field experiment
- c. 180SearchAssistant
- d. Dependent variable

39. A _____ is a collection of symbols, experiences and associations connected with a product, a service, a person or any other artifact or entity.

_____s have become increasingly important components of culture and the economy, now being described as 'cultural accessories and personal philosophies'.

Some people distinguish the psychological aspect of a _____ from the experiential aspect.

- a. Brand equity
- b. Brandable software
- c. Store brand
- d. Brand

40. _____ is a genre of writing that uses fieldwork to provide a descriptive study of human societies. _____ presents the results of a holistic research method founded on the idea that a system's properties cannot necessarily be accurately understood independently of each other. The genre has both formal and historical connections to travel writing and colonial office reports.
- a. ACNielsen
- b. AMAX
- c. ADTECH
- d. Ethnography

41. In the mathematical discipline of graph theory a _____ or edge-independent set in a graph is a set of edges without common vertices. It may also be an entire graph consisting of edges without common vertices.

Given a graph $G = (V,E)$, a _____ M in G is a set of pairwise non-adjacent edges; that is, no two edges share a common vertex.

Chapter 8. Experimentation in Marketing Research

a. 180SearchAssistant
b. Power III
c. 6-3-5 Brainwriting
d. Matching

42. In _____, the population is first segmented into mutually exclusive sub-groups, just as in stratified sampling. Then judgment is used to select the subjects or units from each segment based on a specified proportion. For example, an interviewer may be told to sample 200 females and 300 males between the age of 45 and 60.
   a. Snowball sampling
   b. Quota sampling
   c. Power III
   d. Nonprobability sampling

43. _____ is a broad label that refers to any individuals or households that use goods and services generated within the economy. The concept of a _____ is used in different contexts, so that the usage and significance of the term may vary.

A _____ is a person who uses any product or service.

   a. 180SearchAssistant
   b. Power III
   c. 6-3-5 Brainwriting
   d. Consumer

44. A '_____' or television commercial (often just commercial (US) or advert or ad (UK) or ad-film (India)) is a span of television programming produced and paid for by an organisation that conveys a message. Advertisement revenue provides a significant portion of the funding for most privately owned television networks. The vast majority of _____s today consist of brief advertising spots, ranging in length from a few seconds to several minutes (as well as program-length infomercials.)
   a. Transit media
   b. Ghost sign
   c. Radio commercial
   d. Television advertisement

45. In finance, an _____ is a contract between a buyer and a seller that gives the buyer the right--but not the obligation-- to buy or to sell a particular asset (the underlying asset) at a later day at an agreed price. In return for granting the _____, the seller collects a payment (the premium) from the buyer. A call _____ gives the buyer the right to buy the underlying asset; a put _____ gives the buyer of the _____ the right to sell the underlying asset.
   a. ADTECH
   b. AMAX
   c. ACNielsen
   d. Option

46. _____ is a statistical technique used in market research to determine how people value different features that make up an individual product or service.

The objective of _____ is to determine what combination of a limited number of attributes is most influential on respondent choice or decision making. A controlled set of potential products or services is shown to respondents and by analyzing how they make preferences between these products, the implicit valuation of the individual elements making up the product or service can be determined.

   a. Power III
   b. Likert scale
   c. Semantic differential
   d. Conjoint analysis

47. _____ is a term used to describe a process of preparing and collecting data - for example as part of a process improvement or similar project.

Chapter 8. Experimentation in Marketing Research

_____ usually takes place early on in an improvement project, and is often formalised through a _____ Plan which often contains the following activity.

1. Pre collection activity - Agree goals, target data, definitions, methods
2. Collection - _____
3. Present Findings - usually involves some form of sorting analysis and/or presentation.

A formal _____ process is necessary as it ensures that data gathered is both defined and accurate and that subsequent decisions based on arguments embodied in the findings are valid . The process provides both a baseline from which to measure from and in certain cases a target on what to improve. Types of _____ 1-By mail questionnaires 2-By personal interview

- Six sigma
- Sampling (statistics)

a. Data collection
b. 6-3-5 Brainwriting
c. Power III
d. 180SearchAssistant

Chapter 9. Measurement and Scaling

1. _____ is an advertisement in which a particular product specifically mentions a competitor by name for the express purpose of showing why the competitor is inferior to the product naming it.

This should not be confused with parody advertisements, where a fictional product is being advertised for the purpose of poking fun at the particular advertisement, nor should it be confused with the use of a coined brand name for the purpose of comparing the product without actually naming an actual competitor. ('Wikipedia tastes better and is less filling than the Encyclopedia Galactica.')

In the 1980s, during what has been referred to as the cola wars, soft-drink manufacturer Pepsi ran a series of advertisements where people, caught on hidden camera, in a blind taste test, chose Pepsi over rival Coca-Cola.

   a. Cost per conversion
   b. Heavy-up
   c. Comparative advertising
   d. GL-70

2. _____ is a statistical method used to examine how reliable a test is: A test is performed twice, e.g., the same test is given to a group of subjects at two different times. Each subject should score different than the other subjects, but if the test is reliable then each subject should score the same in both test.

Valentin Rousson, Theo Gasser, and Burkhardt Seifert, (2002) 'Assessing intrarater, interrater and _____ reliability of continuous measurements,' Statistics in Medicine 21:3431-3446.

   a. Power III
   b. Test-retest
   c. 180SearchAssistant
   d. 6-3-5 Brainwriting

3. _____ refer to a collection of facts usually collected as the result of experience, observation or experiment or a set of premises. This may consist of numbers, words particularly as measurements or observations of a set of variables. _____ are often viewed as a lowest level of abstraction from which information and knowledge are derived.
   a. Data
   b. Sample size
   c. Pearson product-moment correlation coefficient
   d. Mean

4. In probability theory and statistics, a _____ is described as the number separating the higher half of a sample, a population from the lower half. The _____ of a finite list of numbers can be found by arranging all the observations from lowest value to highest value and picking the middle one. If there is an even number of observations, the _____ is not unique, so one often takes the mean of the two middle values.
   a. Statistically significant
   b. Frequency distribution
   c. Linear regression
   d. Median

5. _____ is defined by the American _____ Association as the activity, set of institutions, and processes for creating, communicating, delivering, and exchanging offerings that have value for customers, clients, partners, and society at large. The term developed from the original meaning which referred literally to going to market, as in shopping, or going to a market to sell goods or services.

_____ practice tends to be seen as a creative industry, which includes advertising, distribution and selling.

   a. Product naming
   b. Marketing myopia
   c. Customer acquisition management
   d. Marketing

Chapter 9. Measurement and Scaling

6. Consumer market research is a form of applied sociology that concentrates on understanding the behaviours, whims and preferences, of consumers in a market-based economy, and aims to understand the effects and comparative success of marketing campaigns. The field of consumer _____ as a statistical science was pioneered by Arthur Nielsen with the founding of the ACNielsen Company in 1923.

Thus _____ is the systematic and objective identification, collection, analysis, and dissemination of information for the purpose of assisting management in decision making related to the identification and solution of problems and opportunities in marketing.

a. Logit analysis
b. Marketing research
c. Focus group
d. Marketing research process

7. In statistics, _____ is a simple measure of the variability or dispersion of a data set. A low _____ indicates that the data points tend to be very close to the same value (the mean), while high _____ indicates that the data are 'spread out' over a large range of values.

For example, the average height for adult men in the United States is about 70 inches, with a _____ of around 3 inches.

a. Statistically significant
b. Pearson product-moment correlation coefficient
c. Standard deviation
d. Z-test

8. In mathematics and statistics, the arithmetic mean (or simply the mean) of a list of numbers is the sum of all of the list divided by the number of items in the list. If the list is a statistical population, then the mean of that population is called a population mean. If the list is a statistical sample, we call the resulting statistic a _____.

a. Coefficient of variation
b. Z-test
c. Null hypothesis
d. Sample mean

9. In statistics, _____ has two related meanings:

- the arithmetic _____
- the expected value of a random variable, which is also called the population _____.

It is sometimes stated that the '_____' _____s average. This is incorrect if '_____' is taken in the specific sense of 'arithmetic _____' as there are different types of averages: the _____, median, and mode. For instance, average house prices almost always use the median value for the average. These three types of averages are all measures of locations.

a. Confidence interval
b. Standard normal distribution
c. Heteroskedastic
d. Mean

10. A personal and cultural _____ is a relative ethic _____, an assumption upon which implementation can be extrapolated. A _____ system is a set of consistent _____s and measures that is soo not true. A principle _____ is a foundation upon which other _____s and measures of integrity are based.

a. Package-on-Package
b. Value
c. Supreme Court of the United States
d. Perceptual maps

11. _____ or _____ data refers to selected population characteristics as used in government, marketing or opinion research, or the _____ profiles used in such research. Note the distinction from the term 'demography' Commonly-used _____ include race, age, income, disabilities, mobility (in terms of travel time to work or number of vehicles available), educational attainment, home ownership, employment status, and even location.
   a. Albert Einstein
   b. AStore
   c. African Americans
   d. Demographic

12. _____s are used in open sentences. For instance, in the formula x + 1 = 5, x is a _____ which represents an 'unknown' number. _____s are often represented by letters of the Roman alphabet, or those of other alphabets, such as Greek, and use other special symbols.
   a. Personalization
   b. Quantitative
   c. Variable
   d. Book of business

13. _____ is either an activity of a living being (such as a human), consisting of receiving knowledge of the outside world through the senses, or the recording of data using scientific instruments. The term may also refer to any datum collected during this activity.

The scientific method requires _____s of nature to formulate and test hypotheses.

   a. AMAX
   b. ACNielsen
   c. ADTECH
   d. Observation

14. Advertising mail junk mail is the delivery of advertising material to recipients of postal mail. The delivery of advertising mail forms a large and growing service for many postal services, and _____ marketing forms a significant portion of the direct marketing industry. Some organizations attempt to help people opt-out of receiving advertising mail, in many cases motivated by a concern over its negative environmental impact.
   a. Direct mail
   b. Directory Harvest Attack
   c. Telemarketing
   d. Phishing

15. A _____ is a collection of symbols, experiences and associations connected with a product, a service, a person or any other artifact or entity.

_____s have become increasingly important components of culture and the economy, now being described as 'cultural accessories and personal philosophies'.

Some people distinguish the psychological aspect of a _____ from the experiential aspect.

   a. Brandable software
   b. Store brand
   c. Brand equity
   d. Brand

16. _____ refers to the marketing effects or outcomes that accrue to a product with its brand name compared with those that would accrue if the same product did not have the brand name . And, at the root of these marketing effects is consumers' knowledge. In other words, consumers' knowledge about a brand makes manufacturers/advertisers respond differently or adopt appropriately adapt measures for the marketing of the brand .
   a. Product extension
   b. Brand equity
   c. Brand image
   d. Brand aversion

17. _____ is a broad label that refers to any individuals or households that use goods and services generated within the economy. The concept of a _____ is used in different contexts, so that the usage and significance of the term may vary.

A _____ is a person who uses any product or service.

   a. 6-3-5 Brainwriting
   b. Power III
   c. 180SearchAssistant
   d. Consumer

18. _____ psychogalvanic reflex is a method of measuring the electrical resistance of the skin. There has been a long history of electrodermal activity research, most of it dealing with spontaneous fluctuations. Most investigators accept the phenomenon without understanding exactly what it means.
   a. 180SearchAssistant
   b. Power III
   c. Galvanic skin response
   d. 6-3-5 Brainwriting

19. _____ or personalisation is tailoring a consumer product, electronic or written medium to a user based on personal details or characteristics they provide. More recently, it has especially been applied in the context of the World Wide Web.

Web pages are personalized based on the interests of an individual.

   a. Sexism,
   b. Personalization
   c. Flighting
   d. Complex sale

20. _____ are a class of semi-structured projective techniques. _____ typically provide respondents with beginnings of sentences, referred to as 'stems,' and respondents then complete the sentences in ways that are meaningful to them. The responses are believed to provide indications of attitudes, beliefs, motivations, or other mental states.
   a. Reference value
   b. Sentence completion tests
   c. Power III
   d. Response rate

21. The _____ is an example of a projective test.

Historically, the _____ or _____ has been amongst the most widely used, researched, and taught projective psychological tests. Its adherents claim that it taps a subject's unconscious to reveal repressed aspects of personality, motives and needs for achievement, power and intimacy, and problem-solving abilities.

   a. Power III
   b. 6-3-5 Brainwriting
   c. Thematic apperception test
   d. 180SearchAssistant

Chapter 9. Measurement and Scaling 73

22. _____ is a common word game involving an exchange of words that are associated together.

Once an original word has been chosen, usually randomly or arbitrarily, a player will find a word that they associate with it and make it known to all the players, usually by saying it aloud or writing it down as the next item on a list of words so far used. The next player must then do the same with this previous word.

   a. 180SearchAssistant   b. 6-3-5 Brainwriting
   c. Power III   d. Word association

23. _____ is systematic determination of merit, worth, and significance of something or someone using criteria against a set of standards. _____ often is used to characterize and appraise subjects of interest in a wide range of human enterprises, including the arts, criminal justice, foundations and non-profit organizations, government, health care, and other human services.

Depending on the topic of interest, there are professional groups which look to the quality and rigor of the _____ process.

   a. ADTECH   b. Evaluation
   c. AMAX   d. ACNielsen

24. _____ as the name suggests is communication through graphics and graphical aids. It is the process of creating, producing, and distributing material incorporating words and images to convey data, concepts, and emotions.

The field of _____s encompasses all phases of the _____s processes from origination of the idea (design, layout, and typography) through reproduction, finishing and distribution of two- or three-dimensional products or electronic transmissions.

   a. Public relations   b. Symbolic analysis
   c. Power III   d. Graphic communication

25. _____ is one of the four Ps of the marketing mix. The other three aspects are product, promotion, and place. It is also a key variable in microeconomic price allocation theory.
   a. Competitor indexing   b. Price
   c. Relationship based pricing   d. Pricing

26. In grammar, the _____ is the form of an adjective or adverb which denotes the degree or grade by which a person, thing and is used in this context with a subordinating conjunction, such as than, as...as, etc.

The structure of a _____ in English consists normally of the positive form of the adjective or adverb, plus the suffix -er e.g. 'he is taller than his father is', or 'the village is less picturesque than the town nearby'.

   a. 6-3-5 Brainwriting   b. Comparative
   c. Power III   d. 180SearchAssistant

27. _____ was originally coined by Austrian psychologist Alfred Adler in 1929. The current broader sense of the word dates from 1961.

In sociology, a _____ is the way a person lives.

a. 6-3-5 Brainwriting
c. 180SearchAssistant
b. Power III
d. Lifestyle

28. A _____ is a psychometric scale commonly used in questionnaires, and is the most widely used scale in survey research. When responding to a Likert questionnaire item, respondents specify their level of agreement to a statement. The scale is named after its inventor, psychologist Rensis Likert.
   a. Semantic differential
   c. Power III
   b. Factor analysis
   d. Likert Scale

29. The _____ business model is one in which participants bid for products and services over the Internet. The functionality of buying and selling in an auction format is made possible through auction software which regulates the various processes involved.

Several types of _____s are possible.

   a. ADTECH
   c. ACNielsen
   b. AMAX
   d. Online auction

30. _____ is a standard point of view or personal prejudice. especially when the tendency interferes with the ability to be impartial, unprejudiced, or objective. The term _____ed is used to describe an action, judgment, or other outcome influenced by a prejudged perspective.
   a. 6-3-5 Brainwriting
   c. Power III
   b. 180SearchAssistant
   d. Bias

31. In social science and psychometrics, _____ refers to whether a scale measures or correlates with a theorized psychological construct (such as 'fluid intelligence'.) It is related to the theoretical ideas behind the personality trait under consideration; a non-existent concept in the physical sense may be suggested as a method of organising how personality can be viewed. The unobservable idea of a unidimensional easier-to-harder dimension must be 'constructed' in the words of human language and graphics.
   a. Discriminant validity
   c. Predictive validity
   b. Criterion validity
   d. Construct validity

32. In psychometrics, _____ refers to the extent to which a measure represents all facets of a given social construct. For example, a depression scale may lack _____ if it only assesses the affective dimension of depression but fails to take into account the behavioral dimension. An element of subjectivity exists in relation to determining _____, which requires a degree of agreement about what a particular personality trait such as extraversion represents.
   a. Predictive validity
   c. Convergent validity
   b. Criterion validity
   d. Content validity

33. _____ is a property of a test intended to measure something. The test is said to have _____ if it 'looks like' it is going to measure what it is supposed to measure. For instance, if you prepare a test to measure whether students can perform multiplication, and the people you show it to all agree that it looks like a good test of multiplication ability, you have shown the _____ of your test.

a. Selective distortion
c. Power III
b. 180SearchAssistant
d. Face validity

34. In the absence of a more specific context, convergence denotes the approach toward a definite value, as time goes on; or to a definite point, a common view or opinion, or toward a fixed or equilibrium state. _____ is the adjectival form, and also a noun meaning an iterative approximation.

In mathematics, convergence describes limiting behaviour, particularly of an infinite sequence or series, toward some limit.

a. Strict liability
c. Convergent
b. Good things come to those who wait
d. Geo

35. _____ is the degree to which an operation is similar to (converges on) other operations that it theoretically should also be similar to. For instance, to show the _____ of a test of mathematics skills, the scores on the test can be correlated with scores on other tests that are also designed to measure basic mathematics ability. High correlations between the test scores would be evidence of a _____.

a. Criterion validity
c. Discriminant validity
b. Content validity
d. Convergent validity

36. In algebra, the _____ of a polynomial with real or complex coefficients is a certain expression in the coefficients of the polynomial which is equal to zero if and only if the polynomial has a multiple root (i.e. a root with multiplicity greater than one) in the complex numbers. For example, the _____ of the quadratic polynomial

$ax^2 + bx + c$ is $b^2 - 4ac$.

The _____ of the cubic polynomial

$ax^3 + bx^2 + cx + d$ is $b^2c^2 - 4ac^3 - 4b^3d - 27a^2d^2 + 18abcd$.

a. Consumption Map
c. Lifestyle center
b. Discriminant
d. Flighting

37. _____ describes the degree to which the operationalization is not similar to (diverges from) other operationalizations that it theoretically should not be similar to.

Campbell and Fiske (1959) introduced the concept of _____ within their discussion on evaluating test validity. They stressed the importance of using both discriminant and convergent validation techniques when assessing new tests.

a. Criterion validity
c. Convergent validity
b. Discriminant validity
d. Predictive validity

38. A _____ is a statement or claim that a particular event will occur in the future in more certain terms than a forecast. The etymology of this word is Latin . In regards to predicting the future Howard H. Stevenson Says, '_____ is at least two things: Important and hard.' Important, because we have to act, and hard because we have to realize the future we want, and what is the best way to get there.
   a. 6-3-5 Brainwriting
   b. 180SearchAssistant
   c. Power III
   d. Prediction

39. In statistics and research, _____ is a measure based on the correlations between different items on the same test (or the same subscale on a larger test.) It measures whether several items that propose to measure the same general construct produce similar scores. For example, if a respondent expressed agreement with the statements 'I like to ride bicycles' and 'I've enjoyed riding bicycles in the past', and disagreement with the statement 'I hate bicycles', this would be indicative of good _____ of the test.
   a. AMAX
   b. Internal consistency
   c. ACNielsen
   d. ADTECH

40. _____s is the social science that studies the production, distribution, and consumption of goods and services. The term _____s comes from the Ancient Greek oá¼°κονομῖα from oá¼¶κος (oikos, 'house') + vÏŒμος (nomos, 'custom' or 'law'), hence 'rules of the house(hold)'. Current _____ models developed out of the broader field of political economy in the late 19th century, owing to a desire to use an empirical approach more akin to the physical sciences.
   a. Industrial organization
   b. ACNielsen
   c. ADTECH
   d. Economic

41. A _____ is a research instrument consisting of a series of questions and other prompts for the purpose of gathering information from respondents. Although they are often designed for statistical analysis of the responses, this is not always the case. The _____ was invented by Sir Francis Galton.
   a. Mystery shopping
   b. Questionnaire
   c. Mystery shoppers
   d. Market research

Chapter 10. Questionnaire Design

1. _____, a business term, is a measure of how products and services supplied by a company meet or surpass customer expectation. It is seen as a key performance indicator within business and is part of the four perspectives of a Balanced Scorecard.

In a competitive marketplace where businesses compete for customers, _____ is seen as a key differentiator and increasingly has become a key element of business strategy.

   a. Customer satisfaction
   b. Customer base
   c. Supplier diversity
   d. Psychological pricing

2. _____ is the examining of goods or services from retailers with the intent to purchase at that time. _____ is an activity of selection and/or purchase. In some contexts it is considered a leisure activity as well as an economic one.
   a. Shopping
   b. Khodebshchik
   c. Hawkers
   d. Discount store

3. _____ is systematic determination of merit, worth, and significance of something or someone using criteria against a set of standards. _____ often is used to characterize and appraise subjects of interest in a wide range of human enterprises, including the arts, criminal justice, foundations and non-profit organizations, government, health care, and other human services.

Depending on the topic of interest, there are professional groups which look to the quality and rigor of the _____ process.

   a. ACNielsen
   b. AMAX
   c. ADTECH
   d. Evaluation

4. A _____ is a research instrument consisting of a series of questions and other prompts for the purpose of gathering information from respondents. Although they are often designed for statistical analysis of the responses, this is not always the case. The _____ was invented by Sir Francis Galton.
   a. Mystery shopping
   b. Market research
   c. Mystery shoppers
   d. Questionnaire

5. _____ refer to a collection of facts usually collected as the result of experience, observation or experiment or a set of premises. This may consist of numbers, words particularly as measurements or observations of a set of variables. _____ are often viewed as a lowest level of abstraction from which information and knowledge are derived.
   a. Data
   b. Pearson product-moment correlation coefficient
   c. Mean
   d. Sample size

6. _____ is either an activity of a living being (such as a human), consisting of receiving knowledge of the outside world through the senses, or the recording of data using scientific instruments. The term may also refer to any datum collected during this activity.

The scientific method requires _____s of nature to formulate and test hypotheses.

   a. ADTECH
   b. ACNielsen
   c. AMAX
   d. Observation

Chapter 10. Questionnaire Design

7. _____ is that part of statistical practice concerned with the selection of individual observations intended to yield some knowledge about a population of concern, especially for the purposes of statistical inference. Each observation measures one or more properties (weight, location, etc.) of an observable entity enumerated to distinguish objects or individuals.
   a. AStore
   b. Sports Marketing Group
   c. Richard Buckminster 'Bucky' Fuller
   d. Sampling

8. In economics, an externality or spillover of an economic transaction is an impact on a party that is not directly involved in the transaction. In such a case, prices do not reflect the full costs or benefits in production or consumption of a product or service. A positive impact is called an _____ benefit, while a negative impact is called an _____ cost.
   a. ADTECH
   b. ACNielsen
   c. External
   d. AMAX

9. Combining Existing _____ Sources with New Primary Data Sources

Imagine that we could get hold of a good collection of surveys taken in earlier years, such as detailed studies about changes going on in this phase and hopefully additional studies in the years to come. Analyzing this data base over time could give us a good picture of what changes actually have taken place in the orientation of the population and of the extent to which new technical concepts did have an impact on subgroups of the population. Furthermore, data archives can help to prepare studies on change over time by monitoring what questions have been asked in earlier years and alerting principal investigators to important questions which should be repeated in planned research projects.

   a. 180SearchAssistant
   b. Power III
   c. 6-3-5 Brainwriting
   d. Secondary data

10. _____ is a concept that denotes the precise probability of specific eventualities. Technically, the notion of _____ is independent from the notion of value and, as such, eventualities may have both beneficial and adverse consequences. However, in general usage the convention is to focus only on potential negative impact to some characteristic of value that may arise from a future event.
    a. 180SearchAssistant
    b. Risk
    c. Power III
    d. 6-3-5 Brainwriting

11. _____ is a category of response bias in which respondents to a survey have a tendency to agree with all the questions or to indicate a positive connotation.
    a. AMAX
    b. ADTECH
    c. ACNielsen
    d. Acquiescence bias

12. _____ is a standard point of view or personal prejudice. especially when the tendency interferes with the ability to be impartial, unprejudiced, or objective. The term _____ed is used to describe an action, judgment, or other outcome influenced by a prejudged perspective.
    a. Power III
    b. Bias
    c. 6-3-5 Brainwriting
    d. 180SearchAssistant

Chapter 10. Questionnaire Design

13. _____ or _____ data refers to selected population characteristics as used in government, marketing or opinion research, or the _____ profiles used in such research. Note the distinction from the term 'demography' Commonly-used _____ include race, age, income, disabilities, mobility (in terms of travel time to work or number of vehicles available), educational attainment, home ownership, employment status, and even location.
    a. African Americans
    b. AStore
    c. Albert Einstein
    d. Demographic

14. _____ generally refers to a list of all planned expenses and revenues. It is a plan for saving and spending. A _____ is an important concept in microeconomics, which uses a _____ line to illustrate the trade-offs between two or more goods.
    a. 6-3-5 Brainwriting
    b. Power III
    c. 180SearchAssistant
    d. Budget

15. _____ is a term used to describe a process of preparing and collecting data - for example as part of a process improvement or similar project.

    _____ usually takes place early on in an improvement project, and is often formalised through a _____ Plan which often contains the following activity.

    1. Pre collection activity - Agree goals, target data, definitions, methods
    2. Collection - _____
    3. Present Findings - usually involves some form of sorting analysis and/or presentation.

    A formal _____ process is necessary as it ensures that data gathered is both defined and accurate and that subsequent decisions based on arguments embodied in the findings are valid . The process provides both a baseline from which to measure from and in certain cases a target on what to improve. Types of _____ 1-By mail questionnaires 2-By personal interview

    - Six sigma
    - Sampling (statistics)

    a. 180SearchAssistant
    b. 6-3-5 Brainwriting
    c. Power III
    d. Data collection

16. An _____ is a special-purpose computer system designed to perform one or a few dedicated functions, often with real-time computing constraints. It is usually embedded as part of a complete device including hardware and mechanical parts. In contrast, a general-purpose computer, such as a personal computer, can do many different tasks depending on programming.
    a. ADTECH
    b. AMAX
    c. ACNielsen
    d. Embedded system

17. _____ or personalisation is tailoring a consumer product, electronic or written medium to a user based on personal details or characteristics they provide. More recently, it has especially been applied in the context of the World Wide Web.

Web pages are personalized based on the interests of an individual.

a. Flighting
c. Sexism,
b. Personalization
d. Complex sale

18. _____ is a form of promotion that uses the Internet and World Wide Web for the expressed purpose of delivering marketing messages to attract customers. Examples of _____ include contextual ads on search engine results pages, banner ads, Rich Media Ads, Social network advertising, online classified advertising, advertising networks and e-mail marketing, including e-mail spam.

Online video directories for brands are a good example of interactive advertising.

a. ADTECH
c. ACNielsen
b. AMAX
d. Online advertising

19. _____ is a form of communication that typically attempts to persuade potential customers to purchase or to consume more of a particular brand of product or service. 'While now central to the contemporary global economy and the reproduction of global production networks, it is only quite recently that _____ has been more than a marginal influence on patterns of sales and production. The formation of modern _____ was intimately bound up with the emergence of new forms of monopoly capitalism around the end of the 19th and beginning of the 20th century as one element in corporate strategies to create, organize and where possible control markets, especially for mass produced consumer goods.

a. AMAX
c. Advertising
b. ADTECH
d. ACNielsen

20. _____ are used to collect quantitative information about items in a population. Surveys of human populations and institutions are common in political polling and government, health, social science and marketing research. A survey may focus on opinions or factual information depending on its purpose, and many surveys involve administering questions to individuals.

a. Convergent
c. Statistical surveys
b. Gross Margin Return on Inventory Investment
d. BeyondROI

21. _____ refers to the methods, practices and operations conducted to promote and sustain certain categories of commercial activity. The term is understood to have different specific meanings depending on the context. Merchandise is a sale goods at a store

In marketing, one of the definitions of _____ is the practice in which the brand or image from one product or service is used to sell another.

a. New Media Strategies
c. Word of mouth
b. Marketing communication
d. Merchandising

Chapter 11. Sampling Foundations

1. _____ is a sampling technique used when 'natural' groupings are evident in a statistical population. It is often used in marketing research. In this technique, the total population is divided into these groups (or clusters) and a sample of the groups is selected.
   a. Cluster sampling
   b. Power III
   c. Snowball sampling
   d. Quota sampling

2. _____ is anything that is intended to save time, energy or frustration. A _____ store at a petrol station, for example, sells items that have nothing to do with gasoline/petrol, but it saves the consumer from having to go to a grocery store. '_____' is a very relative term and its meaning tends to change over time.
   a. Marketing buzz
   b. Demographic profile
   c. Convenience
   d. MaxDiff

3. _____ is a type of nonprobability sampling which involves the sample being drawn from that part of the population which is close to hand. That is, a sample population selected because it is readily available and convenient. The researcher using such a sample cannot scientifically make generalizations about the total population from this sample because it would not be representative enough.
   a. ADTECH
   b. AMAX
   c. ACNielsen
   d. Accidental sampling

4. Sampling is the use of a subset of the population to represent the whole population. Probability sampling, or random sampling, is a sampling technique in which the probability of getting any particular sample may be calculated. _____ does not meet this criterion and should be used with caution.
   a. Nonprobability sampling
   b. Snowball sampling
   c. Power III
   d. Quota sampling

5. In _____, the population is first segmented into mutually exclusive sub-groups, just as in stratified sampling. Then judgment is used to select the subjects or units from each segment based on a specified proportion. For example, an interviewer may be told to sample 200 females and 300 males between the age of 45 and 60.
   a. Snowball sampling
   b. Quota sampling
   c. Power III
   d. Nonprobability sampling

6. _____ is that part of statistical practice concerned with the selection of individual observations intended to yield some knowledge about a population of concern, especially for the purposes of statistical inference. Each observation measures one or more properties (weight, location, etc.) of an observable entity enumerated to distinguish objects or individuals.
   a. AStore
   b. Richard Buckminster 'Bucky' Fuller
   c. Sports Marketing Group
   d. Sampling

7. In statistics, a simple random sample is a subset of individuals (a sample) chosen from a larger set (a population.) Each individual is chosen randomly and entirely by chance, such that each individual has the same probability of being chosen at any stage during the sampling process, and each subset of k individuals has the same probability of being chosen for the sample as any other subset of k individuals (.) This process and technique is known as _____, and should not be confused with Random Sampling.
   a. Market analysis
   b. Focus group
   c. Logit analysis
   d. Simple random sampling

Chapter 11. Sampling Foundations

8. _____ is a statistical method involving the selection of elements from an ordered sampling frame. The most common form of _____ is an equal-probability method, in which every kth element in the frame is selected, where k, the sampling interval (sometimes known as the 'skip'), is calculated as:

sample size (n) = population size (N) /k

Using this procedure each element in the population has a known and equal probability of selection. This makes _____ functionally similar to simple random sampling.

a. 180SearchAssistant
b. Selection bias
c. Power III
d. Systematic sampling

9. _____ is defined by the American _____ Association as the activity, set of institutions, and processes for creating, communicating, delivering, and exchanging offerings that have value for customers, clients, partners, and society at large. The term developed from the original meaning which referred literally to going to market, as in shopping, or going to a market to sell goods or services.

_____ practice tends to be seen as a creative industry, which includes advertising, distribution and selling.

a. Marketing myopia
b. Product naming
c. Customer acquisition management
d. Marketing

10. Consumer market research is a form of applied sociology that concentrates on understanding the behaviours, whims and preferences, of consumers in a market-based economy, and aims to understand the effects and comparative success of marketing campaigns. The field of consumer _____ as a statistical science was pioneered by Arthur Nielsen with the founding of the ACNielsen Company in 1923 .

Thus _____ is the systematic and objective identification, collection, analysis, and dissemination of information for the purpose of assisting management in decision making related to the identification and solution of problems and opportunities in marketing.

a. Marketing research process
b. Logit analysis
c. Marketing research
d. Focus group

11. _____ is a set of six steps which defines the tasks to be accomplished in conducting a marketing research study. These include problem definition, developing an approach to problem, research design formulation, field work, data preparation and analysis, and report generation and presentation.

a. Market analysis
b. Simple random sampling
c. Marketing research process
d. Preference-rank translation

12. _____ refer to a collection of facts usually collected as the result of experience, observation or experiment or a set of premises. This may consist of numbers, words particularly as measurements or observations of a set of variables. _____ are often viewed as a lowest level of abstraction from which information and knowledge are derived.

a. Pearson product-moment correlation coefficient
b. Mean
c. Sample size
d. Data

Chapter 11. Sampling Foundations

13. _____ is a term used to describe a process of preparing and collecting data - for example as part of a process improvement or similar project.

_____ usually takes place early on in an improvement project, and is often formalised through a _____ Plan which often contains the following activity.

1. Pre collection activity - Agree goals, target data, definitions, methods
2. Collection - _____
3. Present Findings - usually involves some form of sorting analysis and/or presentation.

A formal _____ process is necessary as it ensures that data gathered is both defined and accurate and that subsequent decisions based on arguments embodied in the findings are valid . The process provides both a baseline from which to measure from and in certain cases a target on what to improve. Types of _____ 1-By mail questionnaires 2-By personal interview

- Six sigma
- Sampling (statistics)

a. Data collection
b. 6-3-5 Brainwriting
c. Power III
d. 180SearchAssistant

14. The United States _____ is the government agency that is responsible for the United States Census. It also gathers other national demographic and economic data.
a. Power III
b. 180SearchAssistant
c. Census Bureau
d. 6-3-5 Brainwriting

15. _____ are used to collect quantitative information about items in a population. Surveys of human populations and institutions are common in political polling and government, health, social science and marketing research. A survey may focus on opinions or factual information depending on its purpose, and many surveys involve administering questions to individuals.
a. Gross Margin Return on Inventory Investment
b. BeyondROI
c. Convergent
d. Statistical surveys

16. A sample is a subject chosen from a population for investigation. A _____ is one chosen by a method involving an unpredictable component. Random sampling can also refer to taking a number of independent observations from the same probability distribution, without involving any real population.
a. Random sample
b. 180SearchAssistant
c. Selection bias
d. Power III

17. The _____ is a statistical test used in inference, in which a given statistical hypothesis will be rejected when the value of the statistic is either sufficiently small or sufficiently large. The test is named after the 'tail' of data under the far left and far right of a bell-shaped normal data distribution, or bell curve. However, the terminology is extended to tests relating to distributions other than normal.

a. Power III
b. Sampling error
c. Varimax rotation
d. Two-tailed test

18. Combining Existing _____ Sources with New Primary Data Sources

Imagine that we could get hold of a good collection of surveys taken in earlier years, such as detailed studies about changes going on in this phase and hopefully additional studies in the years to come. Analyzing this data base over time could give us a good picture of what changes actually have taken place in the orientation of the population and of the extent to which new technical concepts did have an impact on subgroups of the population. Furthermore, data archives can help to prepare studies on change over time by monitoring what questions have been asked in earlier years and alerting principal investigators to important questions which should be repeated in planned research projects.

a. Power III
b. 6-3-5 Brainwriting
c. 180SearchAssistant
d. Secondary data

19. _____ are a form of online advertising on the World Wide Web intended to attract web traffic or capture email addresses. It works when certain web sites open a new web browser window to display advertisements. The pop-up window containing an advertisement is usually generated by JavaScript, but can be generated by other means as well.
a. Pop-up ads
b. Customer intelligence
c. Power III
d. Project Portfolio Management

20. 'Speaking generally, properties are those physical quantities which directly describe the physical attributes of the system; _____s are those combinations of the properties which suffice to determine the response of the system. Properties can have all sorts of dimensions, depending upon the system being considered; _____s are dimensionless, or have the dimension of time or its reciprocal.'

The term can also be used in engineering contexts, however, as it is typically used in the physical sciences.

When the terms formal _____ and actual _____ are used, they generally correspond with the definitions used in computer science.

a. Power III
b. 6-3-5 Brainwriting
c. 180SearchAssistant
d. Parameter

21. In probability theory and statistics, _____ indicates the strength and direction of a linear relationship between two random variables. That is in contrast with the usage of the term in colloquial speech, denoting any relationship, not necessarily linear. In general statistical usage, _____ or co-relation refers to the departure of two random variables from independence.
a. Mean
b. Frequency distribution
c. Probability
d. Correlation

22. _____ is one of the four elements of marketing mix. An organization or set of organizations (go-betweens) involved in the process of making a product or service available for use or consumption by a consumer or business user.

The other three parts of the marketing mix are product, pricing, and promotion.

Chapter 11. Sampling Foundations

a. Distribution
b. Comparison-Shopping agent
c. Japan Advertising Photographers' Association
d. Better Living Through Chemistry

23. In statistics, _____ has two related meanings:

- the arithmetic _____
- the expected value of a random variable, which is also called the population _____.

It is sometimes stated that the '_____' _____s average. This is incorrect if '_____' is taken in the specific sense of 'arithmetic _____' as there are different types of averages: the _____, median, and mode. For instance, average house prices almost always use the median value for the average. These three types of averages are all measures of locations.

a. Confidence interval
b. Mean
c. Heteroskedastic
d. Standard normal distribution

24. A personal and cultural _____ is a relative ethic _____, an assumption upon which implementation can be extrapolated. A _____ system is a set of consistent _____s and measures that is soo not true. A principle _____ is a foundation upon which other _____s and measures of integrity are based.

a. Perceptual maps
b. Supreme Court of the United States
c. Value
d. Package-on-Package

25. _____ is the study of the Earth and its lands, features, inhabitants, and phenomena. A literal translation would be 'to describe or write about the Earth'. The first person to use the word '_____' was Eratosthenes.

a. Geography
b. 6-3-5 Brainwriting
c. Power III
d. 180SearchAssistant

26. In mathematics and statistics, the arithmetic mean (or simply the mean) of a list of numbers is the sum of all of the list divided by the number of items in the list. If the list is a statistical population, then the mean of that population is called a population mean. If the list is a statistical sample, we call the resulting statistic a _____.

a. Z-test
b. Null hypothesis
c. Coefficient of variation
d. Sample mean

27. In statistics, a _____ is an interval estimate of a population parameter. Instead of estimating the parameter by a single value, an interval likely to include the parameter is given. Thus, _____s are used to indicate the reliability of an estimate.

a. T-test
b. Confidence interval
c. Sample mean
d. Linear regression

28. In statistics, _____ or estimation error is the error caused by observing a sample instead of the whole population.

An estimate of a quantity of interest, such as an average or percentage, will generally be subject to sample-to-sample variation. These variations in the possible sample values of a statistic can theoretically be expressed as _____s, although in practice the exact _____ is typically unknown.

Chapter 11. Sampling Foundations

a. Varimax rotation
c. Two-tailed test
b. Power III
d. Sampling error

29. _____ can be regarded as an outcome of mental processes (cognitive process) leading to the selection of a course of action among several alternatives. Every _____ process produces a final choice. The output can be an action or an opinion of choice.

a. 180SearchAssistant
c. 6-3-5 Brainwriting
b. Power III
d. Decision making

30. Human beings are also considered to be _____ because they have the ability to change raw materials into valuable _____. The term Human _____ can also be defined as the skills, energies, talents, abilities and knowledge that are used for the production of goods or the rendering of services. While taking into account human beings as _____, the following things have to be kept in mind:

- The size of the population
- The capabilities of the individuals in that population

Many _____ cannot be consumed in their original form. They have to be processed in order to change them into more usable commodities.

a. Power III
c. 180SearchAssistant
b. 6-3-5 Brainwriting
d. Resources

31. In statistics, _____ is a simple measure of the variability or dispersion of a data set. A low _____ indicates that the data points tend to be very close to the same value (the mean), while high _____ indicates that the data are 'spread out' over a large range of values.

For example, the average height for adult men in the United States is about 70 inches, with a _____ of around 3 inches.

a. Statistically significant
c. Pearson product-moment correlation coefficient
b. Z-test
d. Standard deviation

32. The _____ is the number of new cases per unit of person-time at risk. In the same example as above, the _____ is 14 cases per 1000 person-years, because the incidence proportion (28 per 1,000) is divided by the number of years (two.) Using person-time rather than just time handles situations where the amount of observation time differs between people, or when the population at risk varies with time.

a. ACNielsen
c. AMAX
b. ADTECH
d. Incidence rate

33. _____ is the process of finding associated geographic coordinates (often expressed as latitude and longitude) from other geographic data, such as street addresses or the coordinates can be embedded into media such as digital photographs via geotagging.

Reverse _____ is the opposite: finding an associated textual location such as a street address, from geographic coordinates.

a. 6-3-5 Brainwriting
b. Power III
c. Geocoding
d. 180SearchAssistant

Chapter 12. Quality Control and Initial Analysis of Data

1. _____ is a telephone surveying technique in which the interviewer follows a script provided by a software application. The software is able to customize the flow of the questionnaire based on the answers provided, as well as information already known about the participant.

CATI may function in the following manner

- A computerized questionnaire is administered to respondents over the telephone.
- The interviewer sits in front of a computer screen
- Upon command, the computer dials the telephone number to be called.
- When contact is made, the interviewer reads the questions posed on the computer screen and records the respondent's answers directly into the computer.
- Interim and update reports can be compiled instantaneously, as the data are being collected.
- CATI software has built-in logic, which also enhances data accuracy.
- The program will personalize questions and control for logically incorrect answers, such as percentage answers that do not add up to 100 percent.
- The software has built-in branching logic, which will skip questions that are not applicable or will probe for more detail when warranted.

a. 6-3-5 Brainwriting
b. Computer-assisted telephone interviewing
c. Power III
d. 180SearchAssistant

2. _____ refer to a collection of facts usually collected as the result of experience, observation or experiment or a set of premises. This may consist of numbers, words particularly as measurements or observations of a set of variables. _____ are often viewed as a lowest level of abstraction from which information and knowledge are derived.

a. Data
b. Pearson product-moment correlation coefficient
c. Sample size
d. Mean

3. _____ is a process of gathering, modeling, and transforming data with the goal of highlighting useful information, suggesting conclusions, and supporting decision making. _____ has multiple facets and approaches, encompassing diverse techniques under a variety of names, in different business, science, and social science domains.

Data mining is a particular _____ technique that focuses on modeling and knowledge discovery for predictive rather than purely descriptive purposes.

a. 6-3-5 Brainwriting
b. Power III
c. Data analysis
d. 180SearchAssistant

4. _____ was originally coined by Austrian psychologist Alfred Adler in 1929. The current broader sense of the word dates from 1961.

In sociology, a _____ is the way a person lives.

a. 6-3-5 Brainwriting
b. 180SearchAssistant
c. Lifestyle
d. Power III

Chapter 12. Quality Control and Initial Analysis of Data

5. An example of a repeated measures _____ would be if one group were pre- and post-tested. (This example occurs in education quite frequently.) If a teacher wanted to examine the effect of a new set of textbooks on student achievement, (s)he could test the class at the beginning of the year (pretest) and at the end of the year (posttest.)
   a. Moving average
   b. Statistically significant
   c. Null hypothesis
   d. T-test

6. In statistics, an _____ is a term in a statistical model added when the effect of two or more variables is not simply additive. Such a term reflects that the effect of one variable depends on the values of one or more other variables.

Thus, for a response Y and two variables x_1 and x_2 an additive model would be:

$$Y = ax_1 + bx_2 + \text{error}$$

In contrast to this,

$$Y = ax_1 + bx_2 + c(x_1 \times x_2) + \text{error},$$

is an example of a model with an _____ between variables x_1 and x_2 ('error' refers to the random variable whose value by which y differs from the expected value of y.)

   a. Interaction
   b. ADTECH
   c. AMAX
   d. ACNielsen

7. In _____, the population is first segmented into mutually exclusive sub-groups, just as in stratified sampling. Then judgment is used to select the subjects or units from each segment based on a specified proportion. For example, an interviewer may be told to sample 200 females and 300 males between the age of 45 and 60.
   a. Power III
   b. Quota sampling
   c. Nonprobability sampling
   d. Snowball sampling

8. _____ is that part of statistical practice concerned with the selection of individual observations intended to yield some knowledge about a population of concern, especially for the purposes of statistical inference. Each observation measures one or more properties (weight, location, etc.) of an observable entity enumerated to distinguish objects or individuals.
   a. Richard Buckminster 'Bucky' Fuller
   b. Sports Marketing Group
   c. AStore
   d. Sampling

9. A _____ is a research instrument consisting of a series of questions and other prompts for the purpose of gathering information from respondents. Although they are often designed for statistical analysis of the responses, this is not always the case. The _____ was invented by Sir Francis Galton.
   a. Mystery shoppers
   b. Market research
   c. Mystery shopping
   d. Questionnaire

Chapter 12. Quality Control and Initial Analysis of Data

10. An _____ is a special-purpose computer system designed to perform one or a few dedicated functions, often with real-time computing constraints. It is usually embedded as part of a complete device including hardware and mechanical parts. In contrast, a general-purpose computer, such as a personal computer, can do many different tasks depending on programming.

    a. Embedded system   b. ACNielsen
    c. AMAX   d. ADTECH

11. _____ is one of the four elements of marketing mix. An organization or set of organizations (go-betweens) involved in the process of making a product or service available for use or consumption by a consumer or business user.

The other three parts of the marketing mix are product, pricing, and promotion.

    a. Japan Advertising Photographers' Association   b. Comparison-Shopping agent
    c. Better Living Through Chemistry   d. Distribution

12. _____ is an advertisement in which a particular product specifically mentions a competitor by name for the express purpose of showing why the competitor is inferior to the product naming it.

This should not be confused with parody advertisements, where a fictional product is being advertised for the purpose of poking fun at the particular advertisement, nor should it be confused with the use of a coined brand name for the purpose of comparing the product without actually naming an actual competitor. ('Wikipedia tastes better and is less filling than the Encyclopedia Galactica.')

In the 1980s, during what has been referred to as the cola wars, soft-drink manufacturer Pepsi ran a series of advertisements where people, caught on hidden camera, in a blind taste test, chose Pepsi over rival Coca-Cola.

    a. GL-70   b. Heavy-up
    c. Cost per conversion   d. Comparative advertising

13. _____s are used in open sentences. For instance, in the formula $x + 1 = 5$, x is a _____ which represents an 'unknown' number. _____s are often represented by letters of the Roman alphabet, or those of other alphabets, such as Greek, and use other special symbols.

    a. Book of business   b. Personalization
    c. Variable   d. Quantitative

14. _____ is either an activity of a living being (such as a human), consisting of receiving knowledge of the outside world through the senses, or the recording of data using scientific instruments. The term may also refer to any datum collected during this activity.

The scientific method requires _____s of nature to formulate and test hypotheses.

    a. Observation   b. ACNielsen
    c. ADTECH   d. AMAX

Chapter 12. Quality Control and Initial Analysis of Data

15. In statistics, _____ is a collection of statistical models, and their associated procedures, in which the observed variance is partitioned into components due to different explanatory variables. The initial techniques of the _____ were developed by the statistician and geneticist R. A. Fisher in the 1920s and 1930s, and is sometimes known as Fisher's ANOVA or Fisher's _____, due to the use of Fisher's F-distribution as part of the test of statistical significance.

There are three conceptual classes of such models:

1. Fixed-effects models assumes that the data came from normal populations which may differ only in their means. (Model 1)
2. Random effects models assume that the data describe a hierarchy of different populations whose differences are constrained by the hierarchy. (Model 2)
3. Mixed-effect models describe situations where both fixed and random effects are present. (Model 3)

In practice, there are several types of ANOVA depending on the number of treatments and the way they are applied to the subjects in the experiment:

- One-way ANOVA is used to test for differences among two or more independent groups. Typically, however, the One-way ANOVA is used to test for differences among at least three groups, since the two-group case can be covered by a T-test (Gossett, 1908.)

a. Interval estimation
c. Arithmetic mean
b. ACNielsen
d. Analysis of variance

16. _____ are used to describe the basic features of the data gathered from an experimental study in various ways. A _____ is distinguished from inductive statistics. They provide simple summaries about the sample and the measures.

a. Pearson product-moment correlation coefficient
c. Descriptive statistics
b. Frequency distribution
d. P-Value

17. Combining Existing _____ Sources with New Primary Data Sources

Imagine that we could get hold of a good collection of surveys taken in earlier years, such as detailed studies about changes going on in this phase and hopefully additional studies in the years to come. Analyzing this data base over time could give us a good picture of what changes actually have taken place in the orientation of the population and of the extent to which new technical concepts did have an impact on subgroups of the population. Furthermore, data archives can help to prepare studies on change over time by monitoring what questions have been asked in earlier years and alerting principal investigators to important questions which should be repeated in planned research projects.

a. Power III
c. 6-3-5 Brainwriting
b. Secondary data
d. 180SearchAssistant

18. _____ is a mathematical science pertaining to the collection, analysis, interpretation or explanation, and presentation of data. It also provides tools for prediction and forecasting based on data. It is applicable to a wide variety of academic disciplines, from the natural and social sciences to the humanities, government and business.

a. Statistics
b. Type I error
c. Median
d. Null hypothesis

19. In probability theory and statistics, the _____ of a random variable, probability distribution, or sample is a measure of statistical dispersion, averaging the squared distance of its possible values from the expected value (mean.) Whereas the mean is a way to describe the location of a distribution, the _____ is a way to capture its scale or degree of being spread out. The unit of _____ is the square of the unit of the original variable.
a. Variance
b. Correlation
c. Standard deviation
d. Sample size

20. _____ is a term for unprocessed data, it is also known as primary data. It is a relative term _____ can be input to a computer program or used in manual analysis procedures such as gathering statistics from a survey.
a. Product manager
b. Chief marketing officer
c. Raw data
d. Shoppers Food ' Pharmacy

21. _____ is defined by the American _____ Association as the activity, set of institutions, and processes for creating, communicating, delivering, and exchanging offerings that have value for customers, clients, partners, and society at large. The term developed from the original meaning which referred literally to going to market, as in shopping, or going to a market to sell goods or services.

_____ practice tends to be seen as a creative industry, which includes advertising, distribution and selling.

a. Customer acquisition management
b. Marketing myopia
c. Product naming
d. Marketing

22. Consumer market research is a form of applied sociology that concentrates on understanding the behaviours, whims and preferences, of consumers in a market-based economy, and aims to understand the effects and comparative success of marketing campaigns. The field of consumer _____ as a statistical science was pioneered by Arthur Nielsen with the founding of the ACNielsen Company in 1923.

Thus _____ is the systematic and objective identification, collection, analysis, and dissemination of information for the purpose of assisting management in decision making related to the identification and solution of problems and opportunities in marketing.

a. Marketing research process
b. Focus group
c. Logit analysis
d. Marketing research

23. In probability theory and statistics, a _____ is described as the number separating the higher half of a sample, a population from the lower half. The _____ of a finite list of numbers can be found by arranging all the observations from lowest value to highest value and picking the middle one. If there is an even number of observations, the _____ is not unique, so one often takes the mean of the two middle values.
a. Statistically significant
b. Median
c. Linear regression
d. Frequency distribution

Chapter 12. Quality Control and Initial Analysis of Data

24. In statistics, _____ has two related meanings:

- the arithmetic _____
- the expected value of a random variable, which is also called the population _____.

It is sometimes stated that the '_____' _____s average. This is incorrect if '_____' is taken in the specific sense of 'arithmetic _____' as there are different types of averages: the _____, median, and mode. For instance, average house prices almost always use the median value for the average. These three types of averages are all measures of locations.

   a. Heteroskedastic   b. Confidence interval
   c. Standard normal distribution   d. Mean

25. In mathematics and statistics, the arithmetic mean (or simply the mean) of a list of numbers is the sum of all of the list divided by the number of items in the list. If the list is a statistical population, then the mean of that population is called a population mean. If the list is a statistical sample, we call the resulting statistic a _____.
   a. Z-test   b. Coefficient of variation
   c. Null hypothesis   d. Sample mean

26. In statistics, _____ is a simple measure of the variability or dispersion of a data set. A low _____ indicates that the data points tend to be very close to the same value (the mean), while high _____ indicates that the data are 'spread out' over a large range of values.

For example, the average height for adult men in the United States is about 70 inches, with a _____ of around 3 inches.

   a. Standard deviation   b. Pearson product-moment correlation coefficient
   c. Statistically significant   d. Z-test

27. A personal and cultural _____ is a relative ethic _____, an assumption upon which implementation can be extrapolated. A _____ system is a set of consistent _____s and measures that is soo not true. A principle _____ is a foundation upon which other _____s and measures of integrity are based.
   a. Supreme Court of the United States   b. Package-on-Package
   c. Perceptual maps   d. Value

28. _____ or _____ data refers to selected population characteristics as used in government, marketing or opinion research, or the _____ profiles used in such research. Note the distinction from the term 'demography' Commonly-used _____ include race, age, income, disabilities, mobility (in terms of travel time to work or number of vehicles available), educational attainment, home ownership, employment status, and even location.
   a. Demographic   b. AStore
   c. Albert Einstein   d. African Americans

Chapter 12. Quality Control and Initial Analysis of Data

29. In psychology, philosophy, and the cognitive sciences, _____ is the process of attaining awareness or understanding of sensory information. It is a task far more complex than was imagined in the 1950s and 1960s, when it was predicted that building perceiving machines would take about a decade, a goal which is still very far from fruition. The word _____ comes from the Latin words _____, percepio, meaning 'receiving, collecting, action of taking possession, apprehension with the mind or senses.'

_____ is one of the oldest fields in psychology.

a. Power III
c. 180SearchAssistant
b. Groupthink
d. Perception

30. _____ is a broad label that refers to any individuals or households that use goods and services generated within the economy. The concept of a _____ is used in different contexts, so that the usage and significance of the term may vary.

A _____ is a person who uses any product or service.

a. Power III
c. 6-3-5 Brainwriting
b. Consumer
d. 180SearchAssistant

31. _____ is the process of finding associated geographic coordinates (often expressed as latitude and longitude) from other geographic data, such as street addresses or the coordinates can be embedded into media such as digital photographs via geotagging.

Reverse _____ is the opposite: finding an associated textual location such as a street address, from geographic coordinates.

a. Geocoding
c. Power III
b. 6-3-5 Brainwriting
d. 180SearchAssistant

32. _____ is a computer program used for statistical analysis.

_____ (originally, Statistical Package for the Social Sciences) was released in its first version in 1968 after being founded by Norman Nie and C. Hadlai Hull. Nie was then a political science postgraduate at Stanford University, and now Research Professor in the Department of Political Science at Stanford and Professor Emeritus of Political Science at the University of Chicago.

a. 180SearchAssistant
c. Power III
b. 6-3-5 Brainwriting
d. SPSS

33. _____ often refers to either primary or secondary research. Secondary research involves a company using information compiled from various sources, which is about a new or existing product. The advantages of secondary research are that it is relatively cheap and easily accessible.

a. Mystery shoppers
c. Questionnaire
b. Mystery shopping
d. Market research

Chapter 13. Hypothesis Testing

1. _____ is defined by the American _____ Association as the activity, set of institutions, and processes for creating, communicating, delivering, and exchanging offerings that have value for customers, clients, partners, and society at large. The term developed from the original meaning which referred literally to going to market, as in shopping, or going to a market to sell goods or services.

   _____ practice tends to be seen as a creative industry, which includes advertising, distribution and selling.

   a. Marketing
   b. Customer acquisition management
   c. Product naming
   d. Marketing myopia

2. A _____ is a process that can allow an organization to concentrate its limited resources on the greatest opportunities to increase sales and achieve a sustainable competitive advantage. A _____ should be centered around the key concept that customer satisfaction is the main goal.

   A _____ is most effective when it is an integral component of corporate strategy, defining how the organization will successfully engage customers, prospects, and competitors in the market arena.

   a. Societal marketing
   b. Cyberdoc
   c. Psychographic
   d. Marketing strategy

3. A _____ is a plan of action designed to achieve a particular goal.

   _____ is different from tactics. In military terms, tactics is concerned with the conduct of an engagement while _____ is concerned with how different engagements are linked.

   a. Power III
   b. 180SearchAssistant
   c. 6-3-5 Brainwriting
   d. Strategy

4. In probability theory and statistics, _____ indicates the strength and direction of a linear relationship between two random variables. That is in contrast with the usage of the term in colloquial speech, denoting any relationship, not necessarily linear. In general statistical usage, _____ or co-relation refers to the departure of two random variables from independence.
   a. Frequency distribution
   b. Mean
   c. Correlation
   d. Probability

5. 'Speaking generally, properties are those physical quantities which directly describe the physical attributes of the system; _____s are those combinations of the properties which suffice to determine the response of the system. Properties can have all sorts of dimensions, depending upon the system being considered; _____s are dimensionless, or have the dimension of time or its reciprocal.'

   The term can also be used in engineering contexts, however, as it is typically used in the physical sciences.

   When the terms formal _____ and actual _____ are used, they generally correspond with the definitions used in computer science.

a. Power III
b. 6-3-5 Brainwriting
c. 180SearchAssistant
d. Parameter

6. _____ is an advertisement in which a particular product specifically mentions a competitor by name for the express purpose of showing why the competitor is inferior to the product naming it.

This should not be confused with parody advertisements, where a fictional product is being advertised for the purpose of poking fun at the particular advertisement, nor should it be confused with the use of a coined brand name for the purpose of comparing the product without actually naming an actual competitor. ('Wikipedia tastes better and is less filling than the Encyclopedia Galactica.')

In the 1980s, during what has been referred to as the cola wars, soft-drink manufacturer Pepsi ran a series of advertisements where people, caught on hidden camera, in a blind taste test, chose Pepsi over rival Coca-Cola.

a. Heavy-up
b. Cost per conversion
c. GL-70
d. Comparative advertising

7. _____ is marketing based on relationship and value. It may be used to market a service or a product.

Marketing a service-base business is different from marketing a goods-base business.

a. 6-3-5 Brainwriting
b. Power III
c. 180SearchAssistant
d. Services Marketing

8. _____ is a sampling technique used when 'natural' groupings are evident in a statistical population. It is often used in marketing research. In this technique, the total population is divided into these groups (or clusters) and a sample of the groups is selected.
a. Quota sampling
b. Cluster sampling
c. Power III
d. Snowball sampling

9. In statistics, a _____ is an interval estimate of a population parameter. Instead of estimating the parameter by a single value, an interval likely to include the parameter is given. Thus, _____s are used to indicate the reliability of an estimate.
a. Sample mean
b. T-test
c. Linear regression
d. Confidence interval

10. _____ is anything that is intended to save time, energy or frustration. A _____ store at a petrol station, for example, sells items that have nothing to do with gasoline/petrol, but it saves the consumer from having to go to a grocery store. '_____' is a very relative term and its meaning tends to change over time.
a. Demographic profile
b. Marketing buzz
c. MaxDiff
d. Convenience

11. _____ is a type of nonprobability sampling which involves the sample being drawn from that part of the population which is close to hand. That is, a sample population selected because it is readily available and convenient. The researcher using such a sample cannot scientifically make generalizations about the total population from this sample because it would not be representative enough.

Chapter 13. Hypothesis Testing

a. ACNielsen
b. Accidental sampling
c. AMAX
d. ADTECH

12. Sampling is the use of a subset of the population to represent the whole population. Probability sampling, or random sampling, is a sampling technique in which the probability of getting any particular sample may be calculated. _____ does not meet this criterion and should be used with caution.

a. Power III
b. Quota sampling
c. Snowball sampling
d. Nonprobability sampling

13. In _____, the population is first segmented into mutually exclusive sub-groups, just as in stratified sampling. Then judgment is used to select the subjects or units from each segment based on a specified proportion. For example, an interviewer may be told to sample 200 females and 300 males between the age of 45 and 60.

a. Power III
b. Nonprobability sampling
c. Snowball sampling
d. Quota sampling

14. The _____ of a test is a traditional frequentist statistical hypothesis testing concept. In simple cases, it is defined as the probability of making a decision to reject the null hypothesis when the null hypothesis is actually true (a decision known as a Type I error, or 'false positive determination'.) The decision is often made using the p-value: if the p-value is less than the _____, then the null hypothesis is rejected.

a. Standard deviation
b. Statistical hypothesis test
c. Type I error
d. Significance level

15. In statistics, a simple random sample is a subset of individuals (a sample) chosen from a larger set (a population.) Each individual is chosen randomly and entirely by chance, such that each individual has the same probability of being chosen at any stage during the sampling process, and each subset of k individuals has the same probability of being chosen for the sample as any other subset of k individuals (.) This process and technique is known as _____, and should not be confused with Random Sampling.

a. Logit analysis
b. Simple random sampling
c. Market analysis
d. Focus group

16. _____ is a statistical method involving the selection of elements from an ordered sampling frame. The most common form of _____ is an equal-probability method, in which every k^{th} element in the frame is selected, where k, the sampling interval (sometimes known as the 'skip'), is calculated as:

sample size (n) = population size (N) /k

Using this procedure each element in the population has a known and equal probability of selection. This makes _____ functionally similar to simple random sampling.

a. 180SearchAssistant
b. Power III
c. Selection bias
d. Systematic sampling

17. In statistics, the terms _____ and type II error are used to describe possible errors made in a statistical decision process. In 1928, Jerzy Neyman (1894-1981) and Egon Pearson (1895-1980), both eminent statisticians, discussed the problems associated with 'deciding whether or not a particular sample may be judged as likely to have been randomly drawn from a certain population' (1928/1967, p.1): and identified 'two sources of error', namely:

Type I (>α): reject the null-hypothesis when the null-hypothesis is true, and
Type II (>β): fail to reject the null-hypothesis when the null-hypothesis is false

In 1930, they elaborated on these two sources of error, remarking that 'in testing hypotheses two considerations must be kept in view, (1) we must be able to reduce the chance of rejecting a true hypothesis to as low a value as desired; (2) the test must be so devised that it will reject the hypothesis tested when it is likely to be false'

Scientists recognize two different sorts of error:

- Statistical error: the difference between a computed, estimated specified and inherently unpredictable fluctuations in the measurement apparatus or the system being studied.
- Systematic error: the difference between a computed, estimated specified and which, once identified, can usually be eliminated.

Statisticians speak of two significant sorts of statistical error. The context is that there is a 'null hypothesis' which corresponds to a presumed default 'state of nature', e.g., that an individual is free of disease, that an accused is innocent that is, that the individual has the disease, that the accused is guilty, or that the login candidate is an authorized user.

a. Mean
b. Significance level
c. Type I error
d. Probability sampling

18. _____ is one of the four elements of marketing mix. An organization or set of organizations (go-betweens) involved in the process of making a product or service available for use or consumption by a consumer or business user.

The other three parts of the marketing mix are product, pricing, and promotion.

a. Comparison-Shopping agent
b. Better Living Through Chemistry
c. Japan Advertising Photographers' Association
d. Distribution

19. _____ is that part of statistical practice concerned with the selection of individual observations intended to yield some knowledge about a population of concern, especially for the purposes of statistical inference. Each observation measures one or more properties (weight, location, etc.) of an observable entity enumerated to distinguish objects or individuals.

a. Sampling
b. Sports Marketing Group
c. AStore
d. Richard Buckminster 'Bucky' Fuller

20. A personal and cultural _____ is a relative ethic _____, an assumption upon which implementation can be extrapolated. A _____ system is a set of consistent _____s and measures that is soo not true. A principle _____ is a foundation upon which other _____s and measures of integrity are based.

a. Supreme Court of the United States
b. Perceptual maps
c. Value
d. Package-on-Package

Chapter 13. Hypothesis Testing

21. The _____ is a statistical test used in inference, in which a given statistical hypothesis will be rejected when the value of the statistic is either sufficiently small or sufficiently large. The test is named after the 'tail' of data under the far left and far right of a bell-shaped normal data distribution, or bell curve. However, the terminology is extended to tests relating to distributions other than normal.
   a. Sampling error
   b. Power III
   c. Varimax rotation
   d. Two-tailed test

22. A _____, in the field of business and marketing, is a geographic region or demographic group used to gauge the viability of a product or service in the mass market prior to a wide scale roll-out. The criteria used to judge the acceptability of a _____ region or group include:

   1. a population that is demographically similar to the proposed target market; and
   2. relative isolation from densely populated media markets so that advertising to the test audience can be efficient and economical.

The _____ ideally aims to duplicate 'everything' - promotion and distribution as well as `product' - on a smaller scale. The technique replicates, typically in one area, what is planned to occur in a national launch; and the results are very carefully monitored, so that they can be extrapolated to projected national results. The `area' may be any one of the following:

- Television area
- Test town
- Residential neighborhood
- Test site

A number of decisions have to be taken about any _____:

- Which _____?
- What is to be tested?
- How long a test?
- What are the success criteria?

The simple go or no-go decision, together with the related reduction of risk, is normally the main justification for the expense of _____s. At the same time, however, such _____s can be used to test specific elements of a new product's marketing mix; possibly the version of the product itself, the promotional message and media spend, the distribution channels and the price.

   a. Power III
   b. 180SearchAssistant
   c. Preadolescence
   d. Test market

23. _____ refer to a collection of facts usually collected as the result of experience, observation or experiment or a set of premises. This may consist of numbers, words particularly as measurements or observations of a set of variables. _____ are often viewed as a lowest level of abstraction from which information and knowledge are derived.

a. Data
b. Sample size
c. Pearson product-moment correlation coefficient
d. Mean

24. _____ is a way of expressing knowledge or belief that an event will occur or has occurred. In mathematics the concept has been given an exact meaning in _____ theory, that is used extensively in such areas of study as mathematics, statistics, finance, gambling, science, and philosophy to draw conclusions about the likelihood of potential events and the underlying mechanics of complex systems.

a. Heteroskedastic
b. Data
c. Linear regression
d. Probability

25. A _____ is an explicit set of requirements to be satisfied by a material, product, or service.

In engineering, manufacturing, and business, it is vital for suppliers, purchasers, and users of materials, products, or services to understand and agree upon all requirements. A _____ is a type of a standard which is often referenced by a contract or procurement document.

a. Product development
b. New product development
c. Product optimization
d. Specification

26. In mathematics, an _____, or central tendency of a data set refers to a measure of the 'middle' or 'expected' value of the data set. There are many different descriptive statistics that can be chosen as a measurement of the central tendency of the data items.

An _____ is a single value that is meant to typify a list of values.

a. ADTECH
b. ACNielsen
c. AMAX
d. Average

27. Combining Existing _____ Sources with New Primary Data Sources

Imagine that we could get hold of a good collection of surveys taken in earlier years, such as detailed studies about changes going on in this phase and hopefully additional studies in the years to come. Analyzing this data base over time could give us a good picture of what changes actually have taken place in the orientation of the population and of the extent to which new technical concepts did have an impact on subgroups of the population. Furthermore, data archives can help to prepare studies on change over time by monitoring what questions have been asked in earlier years and alerting principal investigators to important questions which should be repeated in planned research projects.

a. 6-3-5 Brainwriting
b. 180SearchAssistant
c. Power III
d. Secondary data

28. _____ is a process of gathering, modeling, and transforming data with the goal of highlighting useful information, suggesting conclusions, and supporting decision making. _____ has multiple facets and approaches, encompassing diverse techniques under a variety of names, in different business, science, and social science domains.

Data mining is a particular _____ technique that focuses on modeling and knowledge discovery for predictive rather than purely descriptive purposes.

a. Power III
c. 6-3-5 Brainwriting
b. 180SearchAssistant
d. Data analysis

29. _____s are used in open sentences. For instance, in the formula x + 1 = 5, x is a _____ which represents an 'unknown' number. _____s are often represented by letters of the Roman alphabet, or those of other alphabets, such as Greek, and use other special symbols.

a. Quantitative
c. Personalization
b. Book of business
d. Variable

30. _____ is a computer program used for statistical analysis.

_____ (originally, Statistical Package for the Social Sciences) was released in its first version in 1968 after being founded by Norman Nie and C. Hadlai Hull. Nie was then a political science postgraduate at Stanford University,and now Research Professor in the Department of Political Science at Stanford and Professor Emeritus of Political Science at the University of Chicago.

a. Power III
c. 6-3-5 Brainwriting
b. 180SearchAssistant
d. SPSS

31. _____ is either an activity of a living being (such as a human), consisting of receiving knowledge of the outside world through the senses, or the recording of data using scientific instruments. The term may also refer to any datum collected during this activity.

The scientific method requires _____s of nature to formulate and test hypotheses.

a. ACNielsen
c. Observation
b. ADTECH
d. AMAX

32. In statistics, _____ is a collection of statistical models, and their associated procedures, in which the observed variance is partitioned into components due to different explanatory variables. The initial techniques of the _____ were developed by the statistician and geneticist R. A. Fisher in the 1920s and 1930s, and is sometimes known as Fisher's ANOVA or Fisher's _____, due to the use of Fisher's F-distribution as part of the test of statistical significance.

There are three conceptual classes of such models:

1. Fixed-effects models assumes that the data came from normal populations which may differ only in their means. (Model 1)
2. Random effects models assume that the data describe a hierarchy of different populations whose differences are constrained by the hierarchy. (Model 2)
3. Mixed-effect models describe situations where both fixed and random effects are present. (Model 3)

In practice, there are several types of ANOVA depending on the number of treatments and the way they are applied to the subjects in the experiment:

- One-way ANOVA is used to test for differences among two or more independent groups. Typically, however, the One-way ANOVA is used to test for differences among at least three groups, since the two-group case can be covered by a T-test (Gossett, 1908.)

a. ACNielsen
b. Arithmetic mean
c. Interval estimation
d. Analysis of variance

33. In probability theory and statistics, the _____ of a random variable, probability distribution, or sample is a measure of statistical dispersion, averaging the squared distance of its possible values from the expected value (mean.) Whereas the mean is a way to describe the location of a distribution, the _____ is a way to capture its scale or degree of being spread out. The unit of _____ is the square of the unit of the original variable.

a. Sample size
b. Standard deviation
c. Correlation
d. Variance

34. A _____ is any statistical hypothesis test in which the test statistic has a chi-square distribution when the null hypothesis is true, or any in which the probability distribution of the test statistic (assuming the null hypothesis is true) can be made to approximate a chi-square distribution as closely as desired by making the sample size large enough.

Some examples of chi-squared tests where the chi-square distribution is only approximately valid:

- Pearson's _____, also known as the chi-square goodness-of-fit test or _____ for independence. When mentioned without any modifiers or without other precluding context, this test is usually understood.
- Yates' _____, also known as Yates' correction for continuity.
- Mantel-Haenszel _____.
- Linear-by-linear association _____.
- The portmanteau test in time-series analysis, testing for the presence of autocorrelation
- Likelihood-ratio tests in general statistical modelling, for testing whether there is evidence of the need to move from a simple model to a more complicated one (where the simple model is nested within the complicated one.)

One case where the distribution of the test statistic is an exact chi-square distribution is the test that the variance of a normally-distributed population has a given value based on a sample variance. Such a test is uncommon in practice because values of variances to test against are seldom known exactly.

If a sample of size n is taken from a population having a normal distribution, then there is a well-known result which allows a test to be made of whether the variance of the population has a pre-determined value.

a. Confounding variables
b. Randomization
c. Type I error
d. Chi-square test

Chapter 13. Hypothesis Testing

35. _____ is one of the four Ps of the marketing mix. The other three aspects are product, promotion, and place. It is also a key variable in microeconomic price allocation theory.
    a. Price
    b. Competitor indexing
    c. Pricing
    d. Relationship based pricing

36. _____ in economics and business is the result of an exchange and from that trade we assign a numerical monetary value to a good, service or asset. If I trade 4 apples for an orange, the _____ of an orange is 4 - apples. Inversely, the _____ of an apple is 1/4 oranges.
    a. Discounts and allowances
    b. Price
    c. Contribution margin-based pricing
    d. Pricing

37. In statistics, _____ has two related meanings:

    - the arithmetic _____
    - the expected value of a random variable, which is also called the population _____.

    It is sometimes stated that the '_____' _____s average. This is incorrect if '_____' is taken in the specific sense of 'arithmetic _____' as there are different types of averages: the _____, median, and mode. For instance, average house prices almost always use the median value for the average. These three types of averages are all measures of locations.

    a. Confidence interval
    b. Standard normal distribution
    c. Heteroskedastic
    d. Mean

38. A _____ is any statistical test for which the distribution of the test statistic under the null hypothesis can be approximated by a normal distribution. Since many test statistics are approximately normally distributed for large samples (due to the central limit theorem), many statistical tests can be performed as approximate _____s if the sample size is not too small. In addition, some statistical tests such as comparisons of means between two samples, or a comparison of the mean of one sample to a given constant, are exact _____s under certain assumptions.
    a. Sample size
    b. Null hypothesis
    c. Confounding variables
    d. Z-test

39. An example of a repeated measures _____ would be if one group were pre- and post-tested. (This example occurs in education quite frequently.) If a teacher wanted to examine the effect of a new set of textbooks on student achievement, (s)he could test the class at the beginning of the year (pretest) and at the end of the year (posttest.)
    a. Null hypothesis
    b. Moving average
    c. Statistically significant
    d. T-test

40. In statistics, _____ is a simple measure of the variability or dispersion of a data set. A low _____ indicates that the data points tend to be very close to the same value (the mean), while high _____ indicates that the data are 'spread out' over a large range of values.

For example, the average height for adult men in the United States is about 70 inches, with a _____ of around 3 inches.

a. Pearson product-moment correlation coefficient
b. Z-test
c. Statistically significant
d. Standard deviation

41. In statistical hypothesis testing, the _____ is the probability of obtaining a result at least as extreme as the one that was actually observed, assuming that the null hypothesis is true. The fact that _____s are based on this assumption is crucial to their correct interpretation.

More technically, a _____ of an experiment is a random variable defined over the sample space of the experiment such that its distribution under the null hypothesis is uniform on the interval [0,1].

a. Correlation
b. Descriptive statistics
c. Pearson product-moment correlation coefficient
d. P-value

42. In psychology, philosophy, and the cognitive sciences, _____ is the process of attaining awareness or understanding of sensory information. It is a task far more complex than was imagined in the 1950s and 1960s, when it was predicted that building perceiving machines would take about a decade, a goal which is still very far from fruition. The word _____ comes from the Latin words _____, percepio, meaning 'receiving, collecting, action of taking possession, apprehension with the mind or senses.'

_____ is one of the oldest fields in psychology.

a. 180SearchAssistant
b. Groupthink
c. Perception
d. Power III

43. _____ is a broad label that refers to any individuals or households that use goods and services generated within the economy. The concept of a _____ is used in different contexts, so that the usage and significance of the term may vary.

A _____ is a person who uses any product or service.

a. 180SearchAssistant
b. Power III
c. 6-3-5 Brainwriting
d. Consumer

Chapter 14. Examining Associations: Correlation and Regression

1. _____s are used in open sentences. For instance, in the formula x + 1 = 5, x is a _____ which represents an 'unknown' number. _____s are often represented by letters of the Roman alphabet, or those of other alphabets, such as Greek, and use other special symbols.
   a. Personalization
   b. Quantitative
   c. Variable
   d. Book of business

2. In statistics, _____ is a collective name for techniques for the modeling and analysis of numerical data consisting of values of a dependent variable and of one or more independent variables The dependent variable in the regression equation is modeled as a function of the independent variables, corresponding parameters, and an error term. The error term is treated as a random variable.
   a. Stepwise regression
   b. Multicollinearity
   c. Variance inflation factor
   d. Regression analysis

3. _____ is a computer program used for statistical analysis.

   _____ (originally, Statistical Package for the Social Sciences) was released in its first version in 1968 after being founded by Norman Nie and C. Hadlai Hull. Nie was then a political science postgraduate at Stanford University,and now Research Professor in the Department of Political Science at Stanford and Professor Emeritus of Political Science at the University of Chicago.

   a. Power III
   b. 6-3-5 Brainwriting
   c. 180SearchAssistant
   d. SPSS

4. In probability theory and statistics, _____ indicates the strength and direction of a linear relationship between two random variables. That is in contrast with the usage of the term in colloquial speech, denoting any relationship, not necessarily linear. In general statistical usage, _____ or co-relation refers to the departure of two random variables from independence.
   a. Frequency distribution
   b. Correlation
   c. Mean
   d. Probability

5. _____ is a form of communication that typically attempts to persuade potential customers to purchase or to consume more of a particular brand of product or service. 'While now central to the contemporary global economy and the reproduction of global production networks, it is only quite recently that _____ has been more than a marginal influence on patterns of sales and production. The formation of modern _____ was intimately bound up with the emergence of new forms of monopoly capitalism around the end of the 19th and beginning of the 20th century as one element in corporate strategies to create, organize and where possible control markets, especially for mass produced consumer goods.
   a. AMAX
   b. ACNielsen
   c. Advertising
   d. ADTECH

6. A _____ is a collection of symbols, experiences and associations connected with a product, a service, a person or any other artifact or entity.

   _____s have become increasingly important components of culture and the economy, now being described as 'cultural accessories and personal philosophies'.

   Some people distinguish the psychological aspect of a _____ from the experiential aspect.

a. Brand
b. Brandable software
c. Store brand
d. Brand equity

7. _____ is one of the four elements of marketing mix. An organization or set of organizations (go-betweens) involved in the process of making a product or service available for use or consumption by a consumer or business user.

The other three parts of the marketing mix are product, pricing, and promotion.

a. Comparison-Shopping agent
b. Distribution
c. Better Living Through Chemistry
d. Japan Advertising Photographers' Association

8. _____ refer to a collection of facts usually collected as the result of experience, observation or experiment or a set of premises. This may consist of numbers, words particularly as measurements or observations of a set of variables. _____ are often viewed as a lowest level of abstraction from which information and knowledge are derived.

a. Pearson product-moment correlation coefficient
b. Mean
c. Sample size
d. Data

9. _____ is one of the four Ps of the marketing mix. The other three aspects are product, promotion, and place. It is also a key variable in microeconomic price allocation theory.

a. Competitor indexing
b. Pricing
c. Price
d. Relationship based pricing

10. An example of a repeated measures _____ would be if one group were pre- and post-tested. (This example occurs in education quite frequently.) If a teacher wanted to examine the effect of a new set of textbooks on student achievement, (s)he could test the class at the beginning of the year (pretest) and at the end of the year (posttest.)

a. Statistically significant
b. Null hypothesis
c. T-TEST
d. Moving average

11. In statistics, _____ is used for two things;

- to construct a simple formula that will predict what value will occur for a quantity of interest when other related variables take given values.
- to allow a test to be made of whether a given variable does have an effect on a quantity of interest in situations where there may be many related variables.

In both cases, several sets of outcomes are available for the quantity of interest together with the related variables.

_____ is a form of regression analysis in which the relationship between one or more independent variables and another variable, called the dependent variable, is modelled by a least squares function, called a _____ equation. This function is a linear combination of one or more model parameters, called regression coefficients. A _____ equation with one independent variable represents a straight line when the predicted value (i.e. the dependant variable from the regression equation) is plotted against the independent variable: this is called a simple _____.

a. Heteroskedastic	b. Sample size
c. Descriptive statistics	d. Linear regression

12. A _____ is a statement or claim that a particular event will occur in the future in more certain terms than a forecast. The etymology of this word is Latin . In regards to predicting the future Howard H. Stevenson Says, ' _____ is at least two things: Important and hard.' Important, because we have to act, and hard because we have to realize the future we want, and what is the best way to get there.

a. Prediction	b. Power III
c. 6-3-5 Brainwriting	d. 180SearchAssistant

13. In algebra, a _____ is a function depending on n that associates a scalar, det(A), to an n×n square matrix A. The fundamental geometric meaning of a _____ is a scale factor for measure when A is regarded as a linear transformation. _____s are important both in calculus, where they enter the substitution rule for several variables, and in multilinear algebra.

For a fixed nonnegative integer n, there is a unique _____ function for the n×n matrices over any commutative ring R. In particular, this function exists when R is the field of real or complex numbers.

a. Package-on-Package	b. Motion Picture Association of America's film-rating system
c. Black Friday	d. Determinant

14. _____ is systematic determination of merit, worth, and significance of something or someone using criteria against a set of standards. _____ often is used to characterize and appraise subjects of interest in a wide range of human enterprises, including the arts, criminal justice, foundations and non-profit organizations, government, health care, and other human services.

Depending on the topic of interest, there are professional groups which look to the quality and rigor of the _____ process.

a. Evaluation	b. AMAX
c. ACNielsen	d. ADTECH

15. A personal and cultural _____ is a relative ethic _____, an assumption upon which implementation can be extrapolated. A _____ system is a set of consistent _____s and measures that is soo not true. A principle _____ is a foundation upon which other _____s and measures of integrity are based.

a. Supreme Court of the United States	b. Package-on-Package
c. Perceptual maps	d. Value

16. In statistics, _____ has two related meanings:

- the arithmetic _____
- the expected value of a random variable, which is also called the population _____.

It is sometimes stated that the '_____' _____s average. This is incorrect if '_____' is taken in the specific sense of 'arithmetic _____' as there are different types of averages: the _____, median, and mode. For instance, average house prices almost always use the median value for the average. These three types of averages are all measures of locations.

a. Confidence interval
b. Standard normal distribution
c. Heteroskedastic
d. Mean

17. _____ is a rivalry between individuals, groups, nations for territory, a niche, or allocation of resources. It arises whenever two or more parties strive for a goal which cannot be shared. _____ occurs naturally between living organisms which co-exist in the same environment.

a. Price fixing
b. Competition
c. Non-price competition
d. Price competition

18. _____ was originally coined by Austrian psychologist Alfred Adler in 1929. The current broader sense of the word dates from 1961.

In sociology, a _____ is the way a person lives.

a. 6-3-5 Brainwriting
b. Lifestyle
c. Power III
d. 180SearchAssistant

19. The terms '_____' and 'independent variable' are used in similar but subtly different ways in mathematics and statistics as part of the standard terminology in those subjects. They are used to distinguish between two types of quantities being considered, separating them into those available at the start of a process and those being created by it, where the latter (_____s) are dependent on the former (independent variables.)

In traditional calculus, a function is defined as a relation between two terms called variables because their values vary.

a. 180SearchAssistant
b. Power III
c. Field experiment
d. Dependent variable

20. _____ is a statistical phenomenon in which two or more predictor variables in a multiple regression model are highly correlated. In this situation the coefficient estimates may change erratically in response to small changes in the model or the data. _____ does not reduce the predictive power or reliability of the model as a whole; it only affects calculations regarding individual predictors.

a. Variance inflation factor
b. Multicollinearity
c. Regression analysis
d. Stepwise regression

21. _____, a business term, is a measure of how products and services supplied by a company meet or surpass customer expectation. It is seen as a key performance indicator within business and is part of the four perspectives of a Balanced Scorecard.

In a competitive marketplace where businesses compete for customers, _____ is seen as a key differentiator and increasingly has become a key element of business strategy.

a. Customer base
b. Psychological pricing
c. Supplier diversity
d. Customer satisfaction

Chapter 15. Overview of Other Multivariate Techniques

1. _____ is a broad label that refers to any individuals or households that use goods and services generated within the economy. The concept of a _____ is used in different contexts, so that the usage and significance of the term may vary.

A _____ is a person who uses any product or service.

   a. Power III
   b. Consumer
   c. 6-3-5 Brainwriting
   d. 180SearchAssistant

2. _____ is a statistical technique used in market research to determine how people value different features that make up an individual product or service.

The objective of _____ is to determine what combination of a limited number of attributes is most influential on respondent choice or decision making. A controlled set of potential products or services is shown to respondents and by analyzing how they make preferences between these products, the implicit valuation of the individual elements making up the product or service can be determined.

   a. Power III
   b. Conjoint analysis
   c. Likert scale
   d. Semantic differential

3. _____ or _____ data refers to selected population characteristics as used in government, marketing or opinion research, or the _____ profiles used in such research. Note the distinction from the term 'demography' Commonly-used _____ include race, age, income, disabilities, mobility (in terms of travel time to work or number of vehicles available), educational attainment, home ownership, employment status, and even location.
   a. Albert Einstein
   b. African Americans
   c. AStore
   d. Demographic

4. The terms '_____' and 'independent variable' are used in similar but subtly different ways in mathematics and statistics as part of the standard terminology in those subjects. They are used to distinguish between two types of quantities being considered, separating them into those available at the start of a process and those being created by it, where the latter (_____s) are dependent on the former (independent variables.)

In traditional calculus, a function is defined as a relation between two terms called variables because their values vary.

   a. Dependent variable
   b. 180SearchAssistant
   c. Field experiment
   d. Power III

5. In the mathematical discipline of graph theory a _____ or edge-independent set in a graph is a set of edges without common vertices. It may also be an entire graph consisting of edges without common vertices.

Given a graph G = (V,E), a _____ M in G is a set of pairwise non-adjacent edges; that is, no two edges share a common vertex.

   a. 180SearchAssistant
   b. Matching
   c. Power III
   d. 6-3-5 Brainwriting

Chapter 15. Overview of Other Multivariate Techniques

6. _____s are used in open sentences. For instance, in the formula x + 1 = 5, x is a _____ which represents an 'unknown' number. _____s are often represented by letters of the Roman alphabet, or those of other alphabets, such as Greek, and use other special symbols.
   a. Personalization
   b. Quantitative
   c. Variable
   d. Book of business

7. _____ involves disseminating information about a product, product line, brand, or company. It is one of the four key aspects of the marketing mix. (The other three elements are product marketing, pricing, and distribution). P>_____ is generally sub-divided into two parts:

   - Above the line _____: Promotion in the media (e.g. TV, radio, newspapers, Internet and Mobile Phones) in which the advertiser pays an advertising agency to place the ad
   - Below the line _____: All other _____. Much of this is intended to be subtle enough for the consumer to be unaware that _____ is taking place. E.g. sponsorship, product placement, endorsements, sales _____, merchandising, direct mail, personal selling, public relations, trade shows

   a. Promotion
   b. Cashmere Agency
   c. Bottling lines
   d. Davie Brown Index

8. An example of a repeated measures _____ would be if one group were pre- and post-tested. (This example occurs in education quite frequently.) If a teacher wanted to examine the effect of a new set of textbooks on student achievement, (s)he could test the class at the beginning of the year (pretest) and at the end of the year (posttest.)
   a. Moving average
   b. Null hypothesis
   c. Statistically significant
   d. T-test

9. In statistics, analysis of variance (_____) is a collection of statistical models, and their associated procedures, in which the observed variance is partitioned into components due to different explanatory variables. In its simplest form _____ gives a statistical test of whether the means of several groups are all equal, and therefore generalizes Student's two-sample t-test to more than two groups.

There are three conceptual classes of such models:

1. Fixed-effects models assumes that the data came from normal populations which may differ only in their means. (Model 1)
2. Random effects models assume that the data describe a hierarchy of different populations whose differences are constrained by the hierarchy. (Model 2)
3. Mixed-effect models describe situations where both fixed and random effects are present. (Model 3)

In practice, there are several types of _____ depending on the number of treatments and the way they are applied to the subjects in the experiment:

   - One-way _____ is used to test for differences among two or more independent groups. Typically, however, the one-way _____ is used to test for differences among at least three groups, since the two-group case can be covered by a T-test (Gossett, 1908.)

Chapter 15. Overview of Other Multivariate Techniques

a. AMAX
b. ADTECH
c. ACNielsen
d. ANOVA

10. _____ is a computer program used for statistical analysis.

_____ (originally, Statistical Package for the Social Sciences) was released in its first version in 1968 after being founded by Norman Nie and C. Hadlai Hull. Nie was then a political science postgraduate at Stanford University, and now Research Professor in the Department of Political Science at Stanford and Professor Emeritus of Political Science at the University of Chicago.

a. 180SearchAssistant
b. 6-3-5 Brainwriting
c. Power III
d. SPSS

11. A personal and cultural _____ is a relative ethic _____, an assumption upon which implementation can be extrapolated. A _____ system is a set of consistent _____s and measures that is soo not true. A principle _____ is a foundation upon which other _____s and measures of integrity are based.

a. Value
b. Package-on-Package
c. Perceptual maps
d. Supreme Court of the United States

12. In statistics, _____ is a collection of statistical models, and their associated procedures, in which the observed variance is partitioned into components due to different explanatory variables. The initial techniques of the _____ were developed by the statistician and geneticist R. A. Fisher in the 1920s and 1930s, and is sometimes known as Fisher's ANOVA or Fisher's _____, due to the use of Fisher's F-distribution as part of the test of statistical significance.

There are three conceptual classes of such models:

1. Fixed-effects models assumes that the data came from normal populations which may differ only in their means. (Model 1)
2. Random effects models assume that the data describe a hierarchy of different populations whose differences are constrained by the hierarchy. (Model 2)
3. Mixed-effect models describe situations where both fixed and random effects are present. (Model 3)

In practice, there are several types of ANOVA depending on the number of treatments and the way they are applied to the subjects in the experiment:

- One-way ANOVA is used to test for differences among two or more independent groups. Typically, however, the One-way ANOVA is used to test for differences among at least three groups, since the two-group case can be covered by a T-test (Gossett, 1908.)

a. ACNielsen
b. Interval estimation
c. Arithmetic mean
d. Analysis of variance

Chapter 15. Overview of Other Multivariate Techniques

13. In probability theory and statistics, the _____ of a random variable, probability distribution, or sample is a measure of statistical dispersion, averaging the squared distance of its possible values from the expected value (mean.) Whereas the mean is a way to describe the location of a distribution, the _____ is a way to capture its scale or degree of being spread out. The unit of _____ is the square of the unit of the original variable.

    a. Variance
    b. Sample size
    c. Correlation
    d. Standard deviation

14. In statistics, an _____ is a term in a statistical model added when the effect of two or more variables is not simply additive. Such a term reflects that the effect of one variable depends on the values of one or more other variables.

Thus, for a response Y and two variables x_1 and x_2 an additive model would be:

$$Y = ax_1 + bx_2 + \text{error}$$

In contrast to this,

$$Y = ax_1 + bx_2 + c(x_1 \times x_2) + \text{error},$$

is an example of a model with an _____ between variables x_1 and x_2 ('error' refers to the random variable whose value by which y differs from the expected value of y.)

    a. ADTECH
    b. AMAX
    c. ACNielsen
    d. Interaction

15. In algebra, the _____ of a polynomial with real or complex coefficients is a certain expression in the coefficients of the polynomial which is equal to zero if and only if the polynomial has a multiple root (i.e. a root with multiplicity greater than one) in the complex numbers. For example, the _____ of the quadratic polynomial

$$ax^2 + bx + c \text{ is } b^2 - 4ac.$$

The _____ of the cubic polynomial

$$ax^3 + bx^2 + cx + d \text{ is } b^2c^2 - 4ac^3 - 4b^3d - 27a^2d^2 + 18abcd.$$

    a. Flighting
    b. Lifestyle center
    c. Consumption Map
    d. Discriminant

16. Linear _____ and the related Fisher's linear discriminant are methods used in statistics and machine learning to find the linear combination of features which best separate two or more classes of objects or events. The resulting combination may be used as a linear classifier, or, more commonly, for dimensionality reduction before later classification.

LDiscriminant analysis is closely related to ANOVA (analysis of variance) and regression analysis, which also attempt to express one dependent variable as a linear combination of other features or measurements.

a. Linear discriminant analysis
b. Discriminant analysis
c. Multiple discriminant analysis
d. Geodemographic segmentation

17. _____ in economics and business is the result of an exchange and from that trade we assign a numerical monetary value to a good, service or asset. If I trade 4 apples for an orange, the _____ of an orange is 4 - apples. Inversely, the _____ of an apple is 1/4 oranges.
   a. Price
   b. Contribution margin-based pricing
   c. Pricing
   d. Discounts and allowances

18. In psychology, philosophy, and the cognitive sciences, _____ is the process of attaining awareness or understanding of sensory information. It is a task far more complex than was imagined in the 1950s and 1960s, when it was predicted that building perceiving machines would take about a decade, a goal which is still very far from fruition. The word _____ comes from the Latin words _____, percepio, meaning 'receiving, collecting, action of taking possession, apprehension with the mind or senses.'

_____ is one of the oldest fields in psychology.

   a. Groupthink
   b. 180SearchAssistant
   c. Power III
   d. Perception

19. _____ are used to describe the basic features of the data gathered from an experimental study in various ways. A _____ is distinguished from inductive statistics. They provide simple summaries about the sample and the measures.
   a. Pearson product-moment correlation coefficient
   b. Frequency distribution
   c. P-Value
   d. Descriptive statistics

20. _____ is a mathematical science pertaining to the collection, analysis, interpretation or explanation, and presentation of data. It also provides tools for prediction and forecasting based on data. It is applicable to a wide variety of academic disciplines, from the natural and social sciences to the humanities, government and business.
   a. Median
   b. Type I error
   c. Statistics
   d. Null hypothesis

21. _____ was originally coined by Austrian psychologist Alfred Adler in 1929. The current broader sense of the word dates from 1961.

In sociology, a _____ is the way a person lives.

   a. 180SearchAssistant
   b. Lifestyle
   c. 6-3-5 Brainwriting
   d. Power III

22. _____ refer to a collection of facts usually collected as the result of experience, observation or experiment or a set of premises. This may consist of numbers, words particularly as measurements or observations of a set of variables. _____ are often viewed as a lowest level of abstraction from which information and knowledge are derived.
   a. Sample size
   b. Mean
   c. Data
   d. Pearson product-moment correlation coefficient

Chapter 15. Overview of Other Multivariate Techniques

23. In statistics, _____ is a simple measure of the variability or dispersion of a data set. A low _____ indicates that the data points tend to be very close to the same value (the mean), while high _____ indicates that the data are 'spread out' over a large range of values.

For example, the average height for adult men in the United States is about 70 inches, with a _____ of around 3 inches.

   a. Z-test
   b. Pearson product-moment correlation coefficient
   c. Statistically significant
   d. Standard deviation

24. _____ is a metric or measure of business performance traditionally associated with sales. Defined as:

Sales can be measured either as the sum of dollars pursued or the number of deals pursued. Accurate calculation requires clear definition of when a sales opportunity is firm enough to be included in the metric, as well as firm disposition of the opportunity (i.e. the deal has reached a point where it is considered won, lost or abandoned.)

   a. Sales management
   b. Lead generation
   c. Sales process
   d. Hit rate

25. _____ is systematic determination of merit, worth, and significance of something or someone using criteria against a set of standards. _____ often is used to characterize and appraise subjects of interest in a wide range of human enterprises, including the arts, criminal justice, foundations and non-profit organizations, government, health care, and other human services.

Depending on the topic of interest, there are professional groups which look to the quality and rigor of the _____ process.

   a. Evaluation
   b. ACNielsen
   c. AMAX
   d. ADTECH

26. In statistics, a result is called _____ if it is unlikely to have occurred by chance. 'A _____ difference' simply means there is statistical evidence that there is a difference; it does not mean the difference is necessarily large, important, or significant in the common meaning of the word.

The significance level of a test is a traditional frequentist statistical hypothesis testing concept.

   a. Standard deviation
   b. Frequency distribution
   c. Randomization
   d. Statistically significant

27. _____ is a statistical method used to describe variability among observed variables in terms of fewer unobserved variables called factors. The observed variables are modeled as linear combinations of the factors, plus 'error' terms. The information gained about the interdependencies can be used later to reduce the set of variables in a dataset.

Chapter 15. Overview of Other Multivariate Techniques

a. Power III
b. Semantic differential
c. Likert scale
d. Factor analysis

28. In probability theory and statistics, _____ indicates the strength and direction of a linear relationship between two random variables. That is in contrast with the usage of the term in colloquial speech, denoting any relationship, not necessarily linear. In general statistical usage, _____ or co-relation refers to the departure of two random variables from independence.
   a. Correlation
   b. Probability
   c. Frequency distribution
   d. Mean

29. In statistics, _____ is used for two things;

   - to construct a simple formula that will predict what value will occur for a quantity of interest when other related variables take given values.
   - to allow a test to be made of whether a given variable does have an effect on a quantity of interest in situations where there may be many related variables.

In both cases, several sets of outcomes are available for the quantity of interest together with the related variables.

_____ is a form of regression analysis in which the relationship between one or more independent variables and another variable, called the dependent variable, is modelled by a least squares function, called a _____ equation. This function is a linear combination of one or more model parameters, called regression coefficients. A _____ equation with one independent variable represents a straight line when the predicted value (i.e. the dependant variable from the regression equation) is plotted against the independent variable: this is called a simple _____.

   a. Descriptive statistics
   b. Sample size
   c. Linear regression
   d. Heteroskedastic

30. '_____' is a class of statistical techniques that can be applied to data that exhibit 'natural' groupings. _____ sorts through the raw data and groups them into clusters. A cluster is a group of relatively homogeneous cases or observations.
   a. 180SearchAssistant
   b. Structure mining
   c. Power III
   d. Cluster analysis

31. In economics, an externality or spillover of an economic transaction is an impact on a party that is not directly involved in the transaction. In such a case, prices do not reflect the full costs or benefits in production or consumption of a product or service. A positive impact is called an _____ benefit, while a negative impact is called an _____ cost.
   a. ADTECH
   b. AMAX
   c. ACNielsen
   d. External

Chapter 15. Overview of Other Multivariate Techniques

32. A _____ is a subgroup of people or organizations sharing one or more characteristics that cause them to have similar product and/or service needs. A true _____ meets all of the following criteria: it is distinct from other segments (different segments have different needs), it is homogeneous within the segment (exhibits common needs); it responds similarly to a market stimulus, and it can be reached by a market intervention. The term is also used when consumers with identical product and/or service needs are divided up into groups so they can be charged different amounts.

   a. Commercial planning
   b. Market segment
   c. Production orientation
   d. Customer insight

33. _____ is a set of related statistical techniques often used in information visualization for exploring similarities or dissimilarities in data. MDS is a special case of ordination. An MDS algorithm starts with a matrix of item-item similarities, then assigns a location to each item in N-dimensional space, where N is specified a priori.

   a. Situational theory of publics
   b. Multidimensional scaling
   c. Cocooning
   d. Convenience

34. In economics, _____ is a measure of the relative satisfaction from consumption of various goods and services. Given this measure, one may speak meaningfully of increasing or decreasing _____, and thereby explain economic behavior in terms of attempts to increase one's _____. For illustrative purposes, changes in _____ are sometimes expressed in units called utils.

   a. AMAX
   b. ADTECH
   c. ACNielsen
   d. Utility

35. _____ is a term used to describe a process of preparing and collecting data - for example as part of a process improvement or similar project.

   _____ usually takes place early on in an improvement project, and is often formalised through a _____ Plan which often contains the following activity.

   1. Pre collection activity - Agree goals, target data, definitions, methods
   2. Collection - _____
   3. Present Findings - usually involves some form of sorting analysis and/or presentation.

   A formal _____ process is necessary as it ensures that data gathered is both defined and accurate and that subsequent decisions based on arguments embodied in the findings are valid. The process provides both a baseline from which to measure from and in certain cases a target on what to improve. Types of _____ 1-By mail questionnaires 2-By personal interview

   - Six sigma
   - Sampling (statistics)

   a. 180SearchAssistant
   b. 6-3-5 Brainwriting
   c. Power III
   d. Data collection

36. In statistics, _____ has two related meanings:

- the arithmetic _____
- the expected value of a random variable, which is also called the population _____.

It is sometimes stated that the '_____' _____s average. This is incorrect if '_____' is taken in the specific sense of 'arithmetic _____' as there are different types of averages: the _____, median, and mode. For instance, average house prices almost always use the median value for the average. These three types of averages are all measures of locations.

a. Confidence interval
c. Mean

b. Heteroskedastic
d. Standard normal distribution

37. _____, a business term, is a measure of how products and services supplied by a company meet or surpass customer expectation. It is seen as a key performance indicator within business and is part of the four perspectives of a Balanced Scorecard.

In a competitive marketplace where businesses compete for customers, _____ is seen as a key differentiator and increasingly has become a key element of business strategy.

a. Psychological pricing
c. Customer base

b. Supplier diversity
d. Customer satisfaction

Chapter 16. Presenting Research Results

1. _____ or _____ data refers to selected population characteristics as used in government, marketing or opinion research, or the _____ profiles used in such research. Note the distinction from the term 'demography' Commonly-used _____ include race, age, income, disabilities, mobility (in terms of travel time to work or number of vehicles available), educational attainment, home ownership, employment status, and even location.

   a. AStore
   b. Demographic
   c. Albert Einstein
   d. African Americans

2. _____ is defined by the American _____ Association as the activity, set of institutions, and processes for creating, communicating, delivering, and exchanging offerings that have value for customers, clients, partners, and society at large. The term developed from the original meaning which referred literally to going to market, as in shopping, or going to a market to sell goods or services.

   _____ practice tends to be seen as a creative industry, which includes advertising, distribution and selling.

   a. Customer acquisition management
   b. Product naming
   c. Marketing
   d. Marketing myopia

3. Consumer market research is a form of applied sociology that concentrates on understanding the behaviours, whims and preferences, of consumers in a market-based economy, and aims to understand the effects and comparative success of marketing campaigns. The field of consumer _____ as a statistical science was pioneered by Arthur Nielsen with the founding of the ACNielsen Company in 1923 .

   Thus _____ is the systematic and objective identification, collection, analysis, and dissemination of information for the purpose of assisting management in decision making related to the identification and solution of problems and opportunities in marketing.

   a. Marketing research process
   b. Focus group
   c. Logit analysis
   d. Marketing research

4. The _____ business model is one in which participants bid for products and services over the Internet. The functionality of buying and selling in an auction format is made possible through auction software which regulates the various processes involved.

   Several types of _____s are possible.

   a. ACNielsen
   b. ADTECH
   c. AMAX
   d. Online auction

5. _____ is a term used in business for a short document that summarises a longer report, proposal or group of related reports in such a way that readers can rapidly become acquainted with a large body of material without having to read it all. It will usually contain a brief statement of the problem or proposal covered in the major document(s), background information, concise analysis and main conclusions. It is intended as an aid to decision making by business managers.

   a. ADTECH
   b. AMAX
   c. ACNielsen
   d. Executive summary

Chapter 16. Presenting Research Results

6. In economics, an externality or spillover of an economic transaction is an impact on a party that is not directly involved in the transaction. In such a case, prices do not reflect the full costs or benefits in production or consumption of a product or service. A positive impact is called an _____ benefit, while a negative impact is called an _____ cost.
   a. ACNielsen
   b. AMAX
   c. External
   d. ADTECH

7. _____ is a term for unprocessed data, it is also known as primary data. It is a relative term _____ can be input to a computer program or used in manual analysis procedures such as gathering statistics from a survey.
   a. Product manager
   b. Shoppers Food ' Pharmacy
   c. Chief marketing officer
   d. Raw data

8. _____ refer to a collection of facts usually collected as the result of experience, observation or experiment or a set of premises. This may consist of numbers, words particularly as measurements or observations of a set of variables. _____ are often viewed as a lowest level of abstraction from which information and knowledge are derived.
   a. Mean
   b. Data
   c. Sample size
   d. Pearson product-moment correlation coefficient

9. _____ is a term used to describe a process of preparing and collecting data - for example as part of a process improvement or similar project.

_____ usually takes place early on in an improvement project, and is often formalised through a _____ Plan which often contains the following activity.

   1. Pre collection activity - Agree goals, target data, definitions, methods
   2. Collection - _____
   3. Present Findings - usually involves some form of sorting analysis and/or presentation.

A formal _____ process is necessary as it ensures that data gathered is both defined and accurate and that subsequent decisions based on arguments embodied in the findings are valid . The process provides both a baseline from which to measure from and in certain cases a target on what to improve. Types of _____ 1-By mail questionnaires 2-By personal interview

- Six sigma
- Sampling (statistics)

   a. 6-3-5 Brainwriting
   b. 180SearchAssistant
   c. Power III
   d. Data collection

10. Combining Existing _____ Sources with New Primary Data Sources

Imagine that we could get hold of a good collection of surveys taken in earlier years, such as detailed studies about changes going on in this phase and hopefully additional studies in the years to come. Analyzing this data base over time could give us a good picture of what changes actually have taken place in the orientation of the population and of the extent to which new technical concepts did have an impact on subgroups of the population. Furthermore, data archives can help to prepare studies on change over time by monitoring what questions have been asked in earlier years and alerting principal investigators to important questions which should be repeated in planned research projects.

a. 6-3-5 Brainwriting
b. Power III
c. 180SearchAssistant
d. Secondary data

11. _____ was originally coined by Austrian psychologist Alfred Adler in 1929. The current broader sense of the word dates from 1961.

In sociology, a _____ is the way a person lives.

a. Power III
b. Lifestyle
c. 6-3-5 Brainwriting
d. 180SearchAssistant

12. _____ is the examining of goods or services from retailers with the intent to purchase at that time. _____ is an activity of selection and/or purchase. In some contexts it is considered a leisure activity as well as an economic one.

a. Khodebshchik
b. Hawkers
c. Shopping
d. Discount store

13. _____ is systematic determination of merit, worth, and significance of something or someone using criteria against a set of standards. _____ often is used to characterize and appraise subjects of interest in a wide range of human enterprises, including the arts, criminal justice, foundations and non-profit organizations, government, health care, and other human services.

Depending on the topic of interest, there are professional groups which look to the quality and rigor of the _____ process.

a. ACNielsen
b. ADTECH
c. Evaluation
d. AMAX

14. A _____ is a research instrument consisting of a series of questions and other prompts for the purpose of gathering information from respondents. Although they are often designed for statistical analysis of the responses, this is not always the case. The _____ was invented by Sir Francis Galton.

a. Mystery shoppers
b. Market research
c. Mystery shopping
d. Questionnaire

15. _____ is a fee paid on borrowed assets. It is the price paid for the use of borrowed money , or, money earned by deposited funds . Assets that are sometimes lent with _____ include money, shares, consumer goods through hire purchase, major assets such as aircraft, and even entire factories in finance lease arrangements.

a. AMAX
b. Interest
c. ACNielsen
d. ADTECH

16. _____, in strategic management and marketing, is the percentage or proportion of the total available market or market segment that is being serviced by a company. It can be expressed as a company's sales revenue (from that market) divided by the total sales revenue available in that market. It can also be expressed as a company's unit sales volume (in a market) divided by the total volume of units sold in that market.

a. Customer relationship management
b. Demand generation
c. Cyberdoc
d. Market share

17. _____ generally refers to a list of all planned expenses and revenues. It is a plan for saving and spending. A _____ is an important concept in microeconomics, which uses a _____ line to illustrate the trade-offs between two or more goods.

a. 6-3-5 Brainwriting
b. Budget
c. Power III
d. 180SearchAssistant

18. _____ is that part of statistical practice concerned with the selection of individual observations intended to yield some knowledge about a population of concern, especially for the purposes of statistical inference. Each observation measures one or more properties (weight, location, etc.) of an observable entity enumerated to distinguish objects or individuals.

a. AStore
b. Sampling
c. Sports Marketing Group
d. Richard Buckminster 'Bucky' Fuller

19. _____ as the name suggests is communication through graphics and graphical aids. It is the process of creating, producing, and distributing material incorporating words and images to convey data, concepts, and emotions.

The field of _____s encompasses all phases of the _____s processes from origination of the idea (design, layout, and typography) through reproduction, finishing and distribution of two- or three-dimensional products or electronic transmissions.

a. Power III
b. Symbolic analysis
c. Public relations
d. Graphic communication

20. In statistics, _____ is a collection of statistical models, and their associated procedures, in which the observed variance is partitioned into components due to different explanatory variables. The initial techniques of the _____ were developed by the statistician and geneticist R. A. Fisher in the 1920s and 1930s, and is sometimes known as Fisher's ANOVA or Fisher's _____, due to the use of Fisher's F-distribution as part of the test of statistical significance.

There are three conceptual classes of such models:

1. Fixed-effects models assumes that the data came from normal populations which may differ only in their means. (Model 1)
2. Random effects models assume that the data describe a hierarchy of different populations whose differences are constrained by the hierarchy. (Model 2)
3. Mixed-effect models describe situations where both fixed and random effects are present. (Model 3)

In practice, there are several types of ANOVA depending on the number of treatments and the way they are applied to the subjects in the experiment:

- One-way ANOVA is used to test for differences among two or more independent groups. Typically, however, the One-way ANOVA is used to test for differences among at least three groups, since the two-group case can be covered by a T-test (Gossett, 1908.)

a. Arithmetic mean
b. Interval estimation
c. ACNielsen
d. Analysis of variance

21. In probability theory and statistics, the _____ of a random variable, probability distribution, or sample is a measure of statistical dispersion, averaging the squared distance of its possible values from the expected value (mean.) Whereas the mean is a way to describe the location of a distribution, the _____ is a way to capture its scale or degree of being spread out. The unit of _____ is the square of the unit of the original variable.

a. Standard deviation
b. Sample size
c. Correlation
d. Variance

22. In statistical hypothesis testing, the _____ is the probability of obtaining a result at least as extreme as the one that was actually observed, assuming that the null hypothesis is true. The fact that _____s are based on this assumption is crucial to their correct interpretation.

More technically, a _____ of an experiment is a random variable defined over the sample space of the experiment such that its distribution under the null hypothesis is uniform on the interval [0,1].

a. Correlation
b. Pearson product-moment correlation coefficient
c. Descriptive statistics
d. P-value

23. A personal and cultural _____ is a relative ethic _____, an assumption upon which implementation can be extrapolated. A _____ system is a set of consistent _____s and measures that is soo not true. A principle _____ is a foundation upon which other _____s and measures of integrity are based.

a. Package-on-Package
b. Supreme Court of the United States
c. Perceptual maps
d. Value

ANSWER KEY

Chapter 1
1. d 2. d 3. d 4. d 5. d 6. d 7. d 8. a 9. a 10. d
11. d 12. a 13. d 14. b 15. d 16. c 17. b 18. b 19. d 20. a
21. d 22. d 23. d 24. d 25. a 26. d 27. d 28. c 29. a 30. b
31. c 32. a 33. c 34. d 35. d 36. d 37. a 38. d 39. d 40. d
41. d 42. c 43. d 44. c 45. c 46. c 47. b

Chapter 2
1. d 2. a 3. a 4. d 5. c 6. b 7. d 8. c 9. d 10. b
11. d 12. d 13. d 14. a 15. a 16. a 17. d 18. d 19. d 20. b
21. b 22. b 23. d 24. c 25. d 26. d 27. b 28. d 29. d 30. b
31. b 32. a 33. a 34. d 35. c 36. b 37. b 38. d 39. b 40. d
41. d 42. b 43. d 44. b 45. d 46. d 47. a 48. d

Chapter 3
1. c 2. d 3. c 4. d 5. b 6. d 7. c 8. d 9. d 10. a
11. d 12. c 13. b 14. d 15. b 16. d 17. c 18. a 19. c 20. d
21. c 22. c 23. d 24. d 25. b 26. a 27. d 28. a 29. a 30. c
31. d

Chapter 4
1. d 2. b 3. d 4. b 5. d 6. a 7. c 8. d 9. b 10. c
11. b 12. c 13. b 14. d 15. d 16. c 17. b 18. d 19. b 20. d
21. d 22. d 23. a 24. b 25. d 26. d 27. a 28. b 29. a 30. a
31. d 32. d 33. d

Chapter 5
1. d 2. c 3. d 4. d 5. a 6. d 7. d 8. d 9. d 10. d
11. a 12. d 13. d 14. a 15. b 16. c 17. d 18. d 19. a 20. d
21. d 22. d 23. d 24. d 25. d 26. d

Chapter 6
1. b 2. c 3. d 4. c 5. b 6. c 7. a 8. b 9. d 10. d
11. a 12. c 13. d 14. c 15. c 16. d 17. b 18. d 19. d 20. a
21. d 22. d 23. a 24. c 25. b 26. c 27. c 28. d 29. b 30. d
31. d 32. a 33. d 34. b 35. a 36. a 37. a 38. c 39. b 40. c
41. d 42. b 43. d 44. b 45. d 46. c

Chapter 7
1. d 2. c 3. a 4. d 5. c 6. d 7. d 8. d 9. d 10. d
11. d 12. c 13. a 14. d 15. a 16. c 17. d 18. d 19. d 20. b
21. d 22. d 23. b 24. b 25. b 26. c 27. d 28. d 29. a 30. d
31. b 32. d

ANSWER KEY

Chapter 8
1. d	2. d	3. c	4. d	5. d	6. a	7. d	8. b	9. d	10. d
11. b	12. d	13. d	14. a	15. d	16. d	17. c	18. b	19. d	20. a
21. d	22. d	23. c	24. d	25. a	26. d	27. d	28. d	29. c	30. d
31. d	32. b	33. d	34. d	35. b	36. c	37. d	38. d	39. d	40. d
41. d	42. b	43. d	44. d	45. d	46. d	47. a			

Chapter 9
1. c	2. b	3. a	4. d	5. d	6. b	7. c	8. d	9. d	10. b
11. d	12. c	13. d	14. a	15. d	16. b	17. d	18. c	19. b	20. b
21. c	22. d	23. b	24. d	25. d	26. b	27. d	28. d	29. d	30. d
31. d	32. d	33. d	34. c	35. d	36. b	37. b	38. d	39. b	40. d
41. b									

Chapter 10
1. a	2. a	3. d	4. d	5. a	6. d	7. d	8. c	9. d	10. b
11. d	12. b	13. d	14. d	15. d	16. d	17. b	18. d	19. c	20. c
21. d									

Chapter 11
1. a	2. c	3. d	4. a	5. b	6. d	7. d	8. d	9. d	10. c
11. c	12. d	13. a	14. c	15. d	16. a	17. d	18. d	19. a	20. d
21. d	22. a	23. b	24. c	25. a	26. d	27. b	28. d	29. d	30. d
31. d	32. d	33. c							

Chapter 12
1. b	2. a	3. c	4. c	5. d	6. a	7. b	8. d	9. d	10. a
11. d	12. d	13. c	14. a	15. d	16. c	17. b	18. a	19. a	20. c
21. d	22. d	23. b	24. d	25. d	26. a	27. d	28. a	29. d	30. b
31. a	32. d	33. d							

Chapter 13
1. a	2. d	3. d	4. c	5. d	6. d	7. d	8. b	9. d	10. d
11. b	12. d	13. d	14. d	15. b	16. d	17. c	18. d	19. a	20. c
21. d	22. d	23. a	24. d	25. d	26. d	27. d	28. d	29. d	30. d
31. c	32. d	33. d	34. d	35. c	36. b	37. d	38. d	39. d	40. d
41. d	42. c	43. d							

Chapter 14
1. c	2. d	3. d	4. b	5. c	6. a	7. b	8. d	9. b	10. c
11. d	12. a	13. d	14. a	15. d	16. d	17. b	18. b	19. d	20. b
21. d									

Chapter 15

1. b	2. b	3. d	4. a	5. b	6. c	7. a	8. d	9. d	10. d
11. a	12. d	13. a	14. d	15. d	16. b	17. a	18. d	19. d	20. c
21. b	22. c	23. d	24. d	25. a	26. d	27. d	28. a	29. c	30. d
31. d	32. b	33. b	34. d	35. d	36. c	37. d			

Chapter 16

1. b	2. c	3. d	4. d	5. d	6. c	7. d	8. b	9. d	10. d
11. b	12. c	13. c	14. d	15. b	16. d	17. b	18. b	19. d	20. d
21. d	22. d	23. d							

www.ingramcontent.com/pod-product-compliance
Lightning Source LLC
Chambersburg PA
CBHW082047230426
43670CB00016B/2807